Bernard N. Wills

I0156357

Believing Weird Things

MINKOWSKI
Institute Press

Bernard N. Wills
Humanities Program
Grenfell Campus
Memorial University of Newfoundland
Corner Brook, NL Canada A2H 6P9

Cover: Image taken from http://de.percyjackson.wikia.com/wiki/Datei:Sphinx.jp

ISBN: 978-1-927763-58-2 (softcover)
ISBN: 978-1-927763-59-9 (ebook)

Minkowski Institute Press
Montreal, Quebec, Canada
http://minkowskiinstitute.org/mip/

For information on all Minkowski Institute Press publications visit our website at http://minkowskiinstitute.org/mip/books/

CONTENTS

ii

PART 1

Part I

1 INTRODUCTION

Recently I read Michael Shermer's book *Why People Believe Weird Things*. I liked it far more than I thought I would. The author is urbane, commands a lucid style, and is rarely if ever shrill or hectoring. He also possesses the scholarly virtue (absent from many recent books in this vein) of adding patient qualifications to the claims he makes. He is rightly impatient with the many forms of quackery on offer in the contemporary world having been, as he relates, a victim of many of them. (2002; 13-15) Dr. Shermer lays the blame for contemporary flim-flam at the feet of three things: magical thinking, pseudo-science, and mysticism. Having diagnosed the illness he then suggests the cure: scientific method which he defines as hypothetico-deductive method. (19) This method he takes to crystalize an attitude he calls skepticism. This is not the kind of skepticism we encounter in the history of philosophy in such works as Cicero's *Academica* or Sextus Empiricus' *Outlines of Pyrrrhonism*. These skeptics are concerned with the necessity and indeed the benefits of the permanent suspension of judgment. Shermer's skepticism rather resembles the methodical skepticism of Descartes (though it is far less radical). It is an attitude of reserve and suspicion we adopt towards claims that are unusual or odd or not part of an established body of knowledge. (16) These are the 'weird' beliefs of the title though Shermer is honest enough to admit the boundaries between 'weird' and 'non-weird' beliefs are of necessity fluid. Helio-centrism was once as weird a belief as creationism is now. Skepticism, as Shermer defines it, must include itself: though we may disdain the beliefs of UFO devotees there is nothing intrinsically impossible about aliens visiting our planet (unless there is something intrinsically impossible about aliens which we are currently incapable of knowing).[1] We must always admit that we

---

[1] If someone claims to have seen or been abducted by U.F.O's I see no way of judging the rationality or irrationality of that belief given that we have no means of estimating the probability or improbability of people from other planets visiting earth or any insight into how they might behave if they did. This topic seems a complete blank slate where judgment is concerned. The best we can do is try assess the overall credibility of the witnesses apart from their specific beliefs about aliens. As I indicate below, I do not find many U.F.0 advocates pass this general smell test but that may be just a personal bias of my own. As one of the earliest commentators on this subject ruefully observed in the 17th Century however "It is hard to resolve this difficulty because we do not yet possess the requisite data" . (Burton, The Anatomy of Melancholy, 2, 55.)

could be proved wrong. (XVII,8,16) Still, well tested beliefs that belong to established and reputable bodies of knowledge are the ones that above all deserve our credence to the exclusion of 'weird' claims like those of astrologers, parapsychologists, palmists and so on.

As an intellectual historian (of sorts) with a background in Classics and philosophy the thing I immediately notice is that almost all the beliefs I study are weird. Aristotle's subtle and beautiful account of soul in the *De Anima* denies that mind is a physical phenomenon which is certainly not the usual position these days. (1941; III, 4, 20-25) Currently I happen to be working through some of the texts in the *Nag Hammadi* library which make claims about the divine origin and destiny of the soul based on what seems like a kind of private illumination or 'gnosis'. In the ancient world Astrology was considered by many to be a well-tested and established body of knowledge and those who doubted its efficacy were outliers (like Christians and Jews) whose objections were often of a religious not a scientific nature. Add to these the tales of the Olympian Gods, the religion of Ancient Egypt, the stories of the Bible, the exploration of transcendent states of consciousness by the Neo-Platonists and you have a whole lot of weird. Far too much 'weird', in fact, to be accounted for by Shermer's catch all explanation 'deficient causal thinking'. With all of these things I find that familiarity dulls my perception of their weirdness. For the most part I can see that they are at very least meaningful and if I can't I can usually find a scholar who can assist me. Sometimes I get to the point of wondering whether, with changes to two or three fundamental assumptions I make about the world, some of these apparently absurd beliefs might become quite plausible. The Ancients do not seem to me to be thinking badly so much as thinking in an alien context and under different assumptions that are too basic to admit evaluation in the ordinary empirical sense (which is *not* to say they admit of no evaluation whatsoever). Further, there are many things in Aristotle and the *Hebrew Bible* which strike me as true even though the question of 'testing' them scientifically and 'skeptically' is pretty much meaningless. In short the weird beliefs I study are at minimum intelligible, sometimes plausible and occasionally true.

It could, of course, be the case that I myself am weird. Maybe contact with Antiquity and with non-Western cultures has so corrupted and clouded my thinking that I cannot tell sense from non-sense. Yet there are things in Shermer's account that give me pause. I will take three of them in turn. Weird beliefs, he indicates, are examples of 'magical thinking'. (Shermer; XXIV) Shermer does not really define this term but from the context it seems to involve a several things. First, it is grounded in our evolved capacity to detect patterns: as it is more beneficial to detect a pattern than it is to miss one this capacity in us is in fact over-developed. (7) We tend to see more patterns than are really there. It also seems to involve a tendency to find causal links where none exist through our capacity for associative thinking. Finally, magical thinking seems to involve wish fulfillment: we see not only patterns that are not there but we have a strong tendency to see patterns that we *want* to see and disregard the things we *don't* want to see. (5) Further, if a man (it seems to be men who drive evolution in Shermer's account) has some success as a shaman or magician he can pass on his genes for magical thinking by getting more or better mates and leaving more offspring. (XXIV) Thus 'magical thinking' becomes a well-established pattern over time.

There are three very immediate problems with this account. Firstly, what evidence is there for a gene for 'magical thinking' such as this account seems to require? Things like magic are transmitted culturally not genetically and hypothesizing a specific genetic predisposition underlying every cultural phenomenon surely violates Occam's razor. We simply have no need of such a hypothesis. Secondly, how do we know that pre-historic societies determined mating relationships on the basis of attractiveness or merit? Many societies *arrange* marriages with little if any thought to the individual qualities of the bride and groom (as opposed to protecting property, cementing alliances and so on). If Shermer knows of any anthropological studies of mating and kinship patterns among the Neanderthals, he should let us know. One feels that Mr. Shermer has here abandoned his usual caution. Thirdly, it is rather hard to see from the description above how magical thinking is distinct from any other thinking: many thought processes having nothing at all to do with magic may be described in terms that Shermer lays out. For instance, many scientists who wish to see a pet theory confirmed see patterns which are not there as in the famous case of Percival Lowell's claim that canals crisscrossed the surface of Mars.

These issues are fairly minor however. My real discomfort comes from the fact that Shermer seems to assume that the origin of 'magical thinking' lies in a cumulative set of inductive misfires. Our putative cave man who enjoys scribbling on a wall notices that several successful hunts have directly followed his artistic outbursts. Remembering these 'hits' more than the misses he has hastily and fallaciously generalized that drawing an animal on a wall makes that animal easier to capture. Thus, magic is causal thinking based on a fallacy of hasty generalization. I actually doubt that even *Homo Erectus* was that crude.[2] However we have many documents from the Classical Greco-Roman world describing magic and the philosophy behind it and it is clear from these that magic is not the simple product of bungled induction. It is in fact the very first form of scientific theorizing. I say this because actual magical thinking (such as we can study in historical

---

[2]One should consider how much acute observation of nature is necessary for two activities Homo Erectus is known to have engaged in; making fire and carving flint. Obviously, there can't have been too much amiss with the inductive powers of early hominids. Indeed, western observers are often incapable of the fine grained observation of natural phenomena that archaic peoples depend on for survival. (Feyerabend, Philosophy of Nature, 22-25) Indeed, there are indigenous peoples today whose classification of botanical types equals or surpasses ours. In domains of interest to them they have many more facts at their command than we do. Of course, the difference between archaic peoples and us has nothing to do with command of the facts. Our early ancestors, perhaps impressed with dynamic process rather than unchanging concepts, encoded their understanding of things human, divine and natural in mythic narratives. We, however, follow the Greek philosophers in encoding our understanding in theories. I cannot deal here with the great question of mythos vs. logos but only note the distinction.

documents) is not simply a set of lazy inductions but a metaphysic and a world view. Magic is closely tied to animism and indeed might be seen as its scientific expression.[3] Animism posits a single living force or power suffused throughout phenomenon (in Greek *dynamis* though the common term among anthropologists is *mana*). Based on this living bond there are occult 'sympathies' (analogical bonds) between various phenomena. Knowing these (and *this* is the inductive part) the magician is able to use these sympathies (or antipathies) to effect desired changes. Thus we have a theoretical structure that supplies us with fundamental physical principles, a set of empirical observations (which actually contained a good deal of precise observation of herbs, minerals and so on) and a practical or technical application of this knowledge. Magic as a scientific system actually outlasted any other ancient form of natural science and did not decisively disappear till the 18th century: in the 17th century Newton (of all people) was still busy about occult researches in alchemy which is the form chemistry takes in the magical world view.

Thus, magic looks for all the world like a science. It is not a science we now employ because we have replaced it with others which are far more precise (being quantitative and not qualitative for instance). Our science has one other advantage: modern scientific knowledge can be expressed in a neutral public way in the language of mathematics. This means anyone at all can learn it whereas magic, even in its most theoretical forms, depends on the charisma and spiritual preparation of the operator. Magic is inherently an elitist doctrine and many texts we have leave crucial gaps in information. One learned magic from practitioners not from books which were only a partial guide. I will happily admit that this is a great improvement. If Mr. Shermer wants to say magic is *bad* science or *outmoded* science he is free to do so. As with any *techne*, magicians probably over promised and under-delivered. He has not, however, convinced me that 'magic' or 'magical thinking' is some inherited capacity *opposed* to science for which more science is the cure. This is simply the propaganda that occurs when one paradigm is replaced by another. The old system becomes the acme of superstition and its practitioners reduced to blundering fools. All the sound observation that went into the old system is forgotten as is its theoretical basis. History, as we are so often reminded, is written by the winners.

My second point concerns pseudo-science, which will come in for a good deal of discussion below. Shermer seems to agree that as a concept 'pseudo-science' is one with fuzzy boundaries. In this it resembles another concept he admits is fuzzy 'scientific method'. (18) However, if it is a problem with weird beliefs that they are pseudo-scientific we might well wonder what it is that makes them so. Shermer answers this question by making a general appeal to scientific beliefs being open to confirmation/disconfirmation: science he tells us is "a set of methods designed to describe and interpret observed or inferred phenomena, past or present, and aimed at building a

---

[3]This is not to say that all or even most magical practices are scientific in intent or form, only that magic has, at various points in its history, taken on such a form.

testable body of knowledge open to rejection or confirmation." (18) [4] Later in his book however he seems to get more specific in a curious discussion of ghosts. This is a race I have no horse in. I'm quite indifferent as to whether there are ghosts or not (as a Christian I base my hope of immortality on divine grace not spooky stories). Mr. Shermer, though, thinks it is very important not to believe in them: "Shouldn't we know by now that ghosts cannot exist unless the laws of science are faulty or incomplete?" (Shermer, 27) This is an odd thing to say as Shermer admits in many other places that all assents to scientific claims are provisional and that science is very much faulty and incomplete. Some scientific laws we thought of as being 'universal' may not apply, for instance, beyond the event horizons of black holes. 'Laws' then can certainly be incomplete. Shermer continues further below: "Ghosts can be considered nonfactual because they have never been confirmed to any extent. Finally, although the law of gravity did not exist before Newton, gravity did. Ghosts never exist apart from their description by believers." (33) Anyone could have said this about the Higgs Boson particle before it was detected. Anyone could have said it about Pluto's moon Charon or the rings of Jupiter. Here Shermer seems to be appealing to some kind of verificationism (and its corresponding notion falsification) to distinguish the scientific concept of gravity from the pseudo-scientific concept of ghosts. Why this is not a tenable position will be outlined below. A further oddity is that Shermer seems to commit one of the fallacies he himself criticizes: that assuming that what exists is what our instruments are currently geared to detect. (48)

However, perhaps Shermer is suggesting something a little different. Perhaps his concern is that belief in ghosts would leave science not accidently or temporarily incomplete but inherently so. Ghosts and spirits appear at least to *suggest* that the system of physical causality is not universal and that there are phenomena that escape its determinism.[5] Nature

---

[4]This will not really serve to distinguish weird and scientific beliefs. Many non-scientific beliefs (including 'weird' ones) can be disconfirmed as easily as scientific ones, like my belief that I will win the lottery next Tuesday or that world will end in 26 days. Some scientific notions cannot (as in current versions of string theory). In any case, scientific theories are constantly being disconfirmed with no loss in their status or prestige: anomalies and aporia are crucial to the progress of any science yet what are these at the end of the day but disconfirmations? Scientific theories (rightly) are resistant to falsification just as much as so called 'superstitions'. These latter can often be falsified, then, and when they are falsified keep right on going in a slightly altered form (just as the sciences often do). This will be discussed more fully below.

[5] Indeed, the suggestion is that 'personalities' are among the things that escape physical determinism at least in part. Relative to disciplines like neuro-science this is a heretical position for in these sciences the connection between mental phenomena and the organic brain is assumed to be intrinsic and necessary. Brains not only CAN support consciousness but ONLY brains can support consciousness. Though Thomists, among others, deny this proposition it can't be said that the Catholic Church, or indeed other mainstream churches, have been friendlier to belief in ghosts. This is because for them spiritualist beliefs, though not necessarily incorrect, are expressions of idle or even dangerous curiosity. Thus, neither western science nor western religion are particularly hospitable to paranormal beliefs as a subject of inquiry (with the exception in the latter case of demonology). This has not stopped and no doubt will never stop popular interest in the subject. This because the ghost will be a vital symbol for ordinary people for as

would not be a closed system and thus we could never be sure whether or not some agent or miraculous power was interfering with it. To be frank, I think this is a problem we are stuck with anyway. The entire realm of culture (the symbolic as opposed to the natural sign) escapes the laws of physical determinism and cannot be explained by it at least in terms of its intentionality: an exhaustive account of the physical universe would not give us even a glimmer of insight into the *meaning* of *Hamlet*. A physical description of a dollar bill would tell us nothing about its use nor would it give us a single principle of economics. Physical determination is a *necessary* but not *sufficient* condition of cultural activity. As Gadamer points out the physicist can only include himself in his equations as a physical object. No equation contains him qua physicist. (1975; 407) Shermer is quite aware of the so called 'demarcation' problem but I do not think he has here escaped it. Apart from a rather vague appeal to verification and falsification (33) he has offered us the suggestion (perhaps?) that only explanations that appeal to physical determinism are valid. This is to ignore that an enormous amount of what we know is based not on experimental reasoning about physical causes such as is typical of the sciences but on interpretive or *hermeneutical* reasoning, the reality of which Mr. Shermer himself admits in the sections of his book that deal with history.[6] Indeed Shermer himself begins his book with some shrewd and insightful comments on the Sermon on the Mount!

Thirdly, Shermer takes issue with something he calls mysticism: "Through the scientific method, we aim for objectivity: basing conclusions on external validation. And we avoid mysticism: basing conclusions on personal insights that elude external validation." (20) Yet it cannot be a problem with 'weird beliefs' that they are incapable of external validation for all

---

long as the burden of the past weighs upon them (and that is forever). Indeed, as the ghost is the most natural of all symbols for the lingering presence of what is past it is difficult to imagine that human beings will ever do without it. If they do their categories for processing experience will be that much poorer for losing an essential metaphor: rewrite Hamlet without ghosts and you will quickly find you have written something else.

[6] As Shermer rightly points out historical claims are open to validation even though they are concerned with singular events rather than general, repeatable laws. (34) This is, of course, because historians have data to appeal to i.e. the records of the past. Historians have the art (perhaps not the science) of constructing narratives about what these records reveal. These narratives are better or worse rather as scientific theories are better or worse: for instance, a good historical account is one that presents the least biased account of an event attainable. This is why hagiography is one thing and history another. Thus we know that at a certain date Caesar crossed the Rubicon. Of course this is not to say that what the historian is concerned with is that a man crossed a body of water: the historian has to include in his account who Caesar was and what his act signified. This narrative element is the essential part of the historian's task because the fact is meaningless without it. Indeed without the explanation it barely makes sense to say there is a fact. The narrative also concerns intentionality and symbolic meaning, the significance of actions and this is where, I believe, the historian's task is very different from the scientist's. The scientist can, of course, considerably increase the amount of data available to the historian and Shermer gives us some interesting examples of this. (38) No science, however, can interpret the facts so uncovered in terms of intentionality and meaning.

kinds of valid knowledge have no external validation. What starlet am I thinking of at the moment? I have entirely objective knowledge of the answer to this question (i.e. I can make of my subjectivity an object of direct reflexive knowledge). You do not know and cannot in principle know that I am thinking of Kirsten Dunst (I could be telling a lie). Moreover of much greater importance than purely subjective facts of this kind is the realm of intersubjective agreement. Many of our experiences we corroborate with others though we cannot validate this knowledge with any external test beyond asking them about *their* internal sensations. Such are our experiences of taste, smell, color and so on. I cannot possibly know that what you see as green I see as green. However, daily experience corroborates for us that our perceptual experiences are closely comparable though the actual subjective experience of another cannot be obtained for comparison or testing.[7] 'Corroboration' (does that look green to you?) while falling short of being an external test in the full sense (where we check some bit of external data observable to both of us) is our fallback form of knowledge in many circumstances. Indeed, many paranormal events (the events at least if not their correct interpretation) *are* corroborated by numbers of people and would thus have to be distinguished from genuine 'mysticism'.

The problem is both simpler and more complex than Shermer realizes. It is not hard to recognize the silliness of truly silly beliefs and a profitless attempt to show that this silliness is a function of such beliefs being 'unscientific' in some methodological sense is hardly necessary. Basic logic, which science shares with every other discipline, is adequate in many cases. Familiarity with a subject area is adequate in others. I do not need any science at all to know that Christopher Marlowe did not write *King Lear*. Anyone who reads this play beside parts one and two of *Tamerlane* can see that they are not by the same author. If they cannot then they should not be reading plays. Sometimes, as with climate change denial, it is simply a question of following the money: climate sceptics are not 'pseudo-scientists' but bought scientists.[8] Sense is separated from nonsense in all kinds of disciplines that do not use or even require scientific method. Bad ideas are not 'pseudo-scientific', 'mystical', or 'magical'. They are simply bad ideas and

---

[7]Science is unable to eliminate trust in subjective reporting or first person knowledge however much it may hedge or limit it. This is evident in fields like medicine where what patients say they feel is sometimes crucial evidence. Indeed, certain over-abstract accounts of 'scientific method' underplay the role first person knowledge and direct observation actually play, the field notes of zoologists being just one example.

[8]Some will assert the reason climate science is not accepted more broadly is that 'post-modernism' and the 'religious right' have eroded trust in the sciences. The real reason it is not accepted however is that oil companies lobby ferociously against it and producer states will not stand up against them. The problem is not 'relativism' but lack of democratic accountability. The issue is political not epistemic. If every single person in North America were a climate change believer this would not change the behavior of fossil fuel corporations or their political stooges one iota. What is more a scientific community that wishes to assert its authority against the corporate sector should be less nakedly subservient to those same corporate interests. It is difficult for scientists who do so much of their work for the corporate sector to turn around and denounce the same corporations as the greatest threat to the planet.

different domains of knowledge have their own ways of determining which ideas fall in this category.

In another way, though, the question is more complex. Many weird ideas are only weird from a certain assumed perspective. This is important because this assumed perspective is often one of epistemic and social privilege. We tend to associate weird ideas with weird people we look down upon from some place of superior social status. One doesn't need to talk to certain humanists very long to realize that by 'Christian' they do not mean Meister Eckhart or Bach. Indeed, a friend of mine once told me that she was raised not a Christian but a Catholic! Clearly 'Christian' is being used here to denote not a historical tradition but a current regional or social identity. Generally, a regional or social identity the speaker is eager to dissociate herself from. God, far from being one of the fundamental concepts of Western metaphysics, is something only semi-literates from Alabama believe in. Other weird beliefs are in fact folk beliefs. Folk beliefs look strange if you are not a folk.[9] Indeed, if we are not folk we tend to call them superstitions. If one adds to this racial and national difference the contempt only deepens: thus we have quite sophisticated religious systems like Voodoo routinely invoked as the acme of superstition.[10] It ought to give us pause that we denigrate so casually the beliefs of people we oppress and victimize at the very same time: the relationship of 'enlightened' western countries to Haiti is a litany of shame. That certain Haitians may cling to their own indigenous beliefs rather than those of their Western oppressors is hardly surprising: in the 18th Century Haitians dared to embrace the Enlightenment and we have not stopped punishing them since. Familiarity however breeds understanding. None of the beliefs mentioned above or below, whether true or false, are anywhere near as irrational as the self-appointed defenders of reason pretend. As Bruno Latour reminds us: "Instead of looking for explanations as to why people hold strange be-

---

[9]I recall a passage in Virgil's Georgics (III, 271-82) where he mentions that mares can be impregnated by the wind. On one level of course this reflects the fact that horses are very 'windy'. The wind and a horse share the nature of being swift and impulsive and difficult to control. To say the horse is born of the wind is simply one way of expressing this commonality of form. This presents no problem to the folk mind for of course the horse breeder who holds this belief pursues all ordinary means of horse-breeding as well with little sense of conflict or contradiction. The folk belief, in fact, is drawing a rough distinction between what Aristotle would call efficient and formal causality, the first being the action of the stallion and the second the inner nature or form of the horse.

[10]At what level do Voudoun actually differ from western scientists? They believe that certain drugs accompanied by certain ritual gestures can render a person catatonic. Western scientists like Wade Davis believe the same thing. They do not differ at all about the extension of the term 'zombie': they agree on what objects we should call zombies. However, they do disagree on what a zombie is. Or do they? If pressed one would qualify the power of suggestion that creates a zombie as 'magical' the other as 'psychological'. Does this reflect anything deeper than the fact that the first lives in Haiti and the second lives in North America? I suppose the scientist would say that zombies are a 'psychological' phenomenon because zombification is produced by natural forces immanent to the subject. But does the Voudoun actually deny this? The difference seems to lie at the descriptive level: the language used to talk about zombies. At the end of a thick description we might just find the referents of each language system to be roughly the same.

liefs, the first thing to do, when told the many stories about someone else's irrationality, is to try and reverse their outcome." (1998; 190)[11]

This is what the essays in this volume will be devoted to showing. There are indeed 'weird' beliefs if by this one means beliefs that are irrational to hold or morally repugnant. As Shermer himself eloquently shows (in one of the best chapters in his book) holocaust denial is one of these beliefs, a belief grounded in contempt for evidence and racial hatred. Judging the 'weirdness' of beliefs takes the kind of practiced eye that criticizing a painting does. On the other hand many other weird beliefs have a good deal to be said for them. Below I shall examine a number of these from the fringes of science and religion to folklore and myth. I don't do so in every instance as a believer: ideas can be interesting and informative without necessarily being true. Nor do I expect or even want to convert anybody. My interest is in a healthy (as opposed to an unhealthy) pluralism consistent with inhabiting a global society that contains a plurality of perspectives as an irreducible feature. This does not preclude judgment: there is plenty to be said *against* certain things. There are beliefs like racism which can only become plausible if we shut down our human capacity for empathy. Further (as we shall see below) others involve deliberate blindness to relevant data: there are beliefs which are *ideological* in character which is to say that they are constructions that mask privilege and power. In such constructions manifest contradictions are papered over and evident facts suppressed. With all the good will in the world we cannot escape the conclusion that *deconstruction* of certain positions is a necessary task. This is especially the case as ideological constructions often have highly paid and articulate spokesmen whereas things like folk beliefs do not.[12]

Accordingly, the first section of this book will explore some subjects which are *outré* where standard epistemology is concerned. We will explore the beliefs of astrologers, people who encounter fairies and eccentric religious positions such as those of the Rastafarians. I will explore other topics such as the existence of god which are certainly respectable from the standpoint of the philosophical tradition but are not so from the viewpoint of many contemporaries who espouse a view we might call 'naturalism'.

---

[11] Everybody has some story to tell about someone else's lack of reason or basic thinking skills yet we rarely stop and test these stories. In a manner reminiscent of the tropes of the Ancient Skeptics, Latour offers us four strategies for doing so. Firstly, we might recast the story of the accused's irrationality as a story about the accuser: an Azande anthropologist observing the English could find many out and out absurdities that make Azande beliefs look sane in comparison. Secondly, we can put the beliefs of others in a context that makes them more comprehensible. Thirdly, we can tell a longer story in which many irrational or contradictory outcomes follow from behavior or principles supposed consistent and rational. Fourthly, we might simply point out that many of the contradictions present in the other's beliefs are present in our putative knowledge. (190) Whatever one thinks of Latour's overall account of science and society these are all healthy skeptical exercises.

[12] Medieval farmers used to place consecrated hosts among their livestock. This kind of thing has always been denounced by the theological class as corruption. The theological class, however, has rarely had to worry about livestock. I am quite happy to think that the medieval farmer has simply found a quirky (to us) way of asking for his daily bread. (see Kiekhefer, Magic in the Middle Ages, 79)

Indeed, if we might be frank about the weirdness of weird beliefs it seems (in many cases) to be that they present (or at least are *thought* to present) at least an implicit challenge to this latter viewpoint. Indeed, 'weird' beliefs are often grounded in stances, such as religious ones, whose roots lie in the pre-modern world. Such beliefs have been confined to the dustbin of history a thousand times over only to re-emerge in some more virulent or irrational form, which ought to give us pause concerning whether our secular self-confidence may in fact be secular arrogance.

In the second section we will explore not only the nature of 'bad' ideological beliefs that are demonstrably false and destructive but also respectable ideas, like the efficacy of violence, which perhaps should be considered weird. We will also deal with the question of tolerance which has been an implicit question in most of the essays of this book. I argue that certain beliefs should be given more tolerance than they are but that others should be given less so the reader will naturally want to know how I draw this line. The reader will note, no doubt, that the tone of this book changes considerably in the second half. This reflects the pressure of events as the author has become more and more concerned with addressing the rising current of extremism in Western politics: a current whose visible expression is certainly NOT worthy of tolerance though many of those swept up in it have legitimate grievances that must be attended to. This has led the author to a reconsideration of Marx (who suddenly seems not nearly so 'weird' as he did at the end of the last century). Thus, I have appended a final pair of essays dealing with the 'irrational' currents in contemporary politics some of which present themselves under quite respectable forms. I append this piece because it is necessary to remind ourselves that from the secure standpoint of an achieved critical culture it is easy to look with tolerance and understanding on the eccentric beliefs and practices of others. Many people, and Mr. Shermer would surely be among them, legitimately fear that we are losing or have lost such a culture and that we must therefore draw a line in the sand concerning anything that smacks of the non or supra rational. I don't think such lines in the sand are truly effective (or they would have worked long ago) however much I appreciate the sentiment. The excluded will avenge itself as Euripides taught us in the *Bacchae*. That said Neo-liberalism and Fascism are far more destructive superstitions than astrology or animism, belief in which may in some respects be far more rational than the Faustian delusions of left and rightwing technocrats. They are *ideologies* not eccentric life-options that can exist in a free society as they threaten both that society and the very physical basis on which it rests. It is for this reason that these 'magical thinkers' will be subjected to strenuous critique though I have been comparatively gentle to others. To conclude, I would like to thank my late colleague Dr. Darren Hynes whose critical eye would have made this book so much better than it is.

2 ASTROLOGY: SCIENCE OR PSEUDO-SCIENCE? THE CHALLENGE OF DEMARCATION

The sciences (or at least the philosophy of science) are in an odd state. There is hardly any discipline so serenely certain of its boundaries. On the inside are studies like zoology, botany, chemistry, physics, micro-biology and so on. A few studies, like exo-biology, are perhaps edging close to the border of something non-scientific but this induces no great concern or worry. If the scientific community is well assured as to what belongs inside of its domain it is equally sure as to what belongs outside of it. It even has a label for studies like astrology, creation science, homeopathy, parapsychology and cognate areas of interest: it calls them pseudo-science. By this it does not mean to call them BAD science (of which there is a great deal) but not science at all. Moreover, the phrase is not intended as a compliment. Pseudoscience is not only NOT science it is also an intellectual pathology. Pseudoscientists suffer from gullibility, magical thinking, wishful thinking etc. if they are not actual charlatans. Pseudo-science differs from science first and foremost in being grounded in an epistemic vice. It differs as well in not following appropriate scientific method so that we can define its viciousness not only in moral terms but in terms of its violation of sound canons of scientific thinking.

Here however, is where things get interesting. While science agrees as to the extension of the term pseudo-science (we all agree as to what things are pseudo-sciences) there seems little to no consensus, alas, as to what makes them so. The intension of the term seems entirely up for grabs. In philosophy of science this is known as the demarcation problem and few think it has been adequately resolved. The problem is that almost all of the proposed criteria for a pseudo-science entail chopping off some branch of legitimate science with it. Similarly, any criteria broad enough to include all aspects of science currently regarded as legitimate seem to include some pseudoscience as well. Thus, it is has proved very hard to say what specific canons of scientific method pseudo-science violates. In the case of astrology, a long-standing *bête noir* of those who oppose the evils of pseudo-science, the case is even worse. Astrology has been attacked for being too 'theoretical' and having no empirical basis. It has also been attacked (by the followers of Kuhn) for being too bluntly empirical and generating no sophisticated theories or clever problem solving. It has been attacked by on the grounds that its claims have been empirically falsified. It has also been attacked (by Popper and co.) on the grounds that its claims are un-falsifiable. It would not surprise me if someone somewhere has attacked it on both grounds at once![13] *You Tube* is now replete with 'refutations' of Astrology from the likes of Dawkins, Hitchens (of all people), James Randi and even Bill Nye the science guy. All of these are scornful and/or angry in tone. They also share the property, related no doubt, of being quite empty of substance.

It is a bit puzzling that Astrology should be attacked for such a variety of contradictory reasons. Clearly, Astrology is not acceptable to modern students of science on an intuitive level however much they may differ on why this is so. Accordingly, I will spend the next little while inquiring into the nature of astrology and trying to define what renders it a pseudo-science, or, if this term is too polemical and moralistic, a non-science. Hopefully, this inquiry will shed some broader light on the problem of demarcation and give us some sense of why practices like Astrology are objects of opprobrium rather than curiosity for so many of the educated. In other words, I am trying to convey how it is that in practice legitimate sciences are demarcated using the notorious case of Astrology as my paradigm. Why is it that Astrologers, once at the center of culture, are now a sub-culture relegated to the margins on a par with Kirilian photographers or people who believe themselves to be Jedi knights?

I will begin with some general observations. Firstly, let me note that that before the 17th century Astrology was broadly (if not universally) accepted as a science. Indeed, some (as we shall see below) would argue that it was indeed, at that time, a science. I am inclined to think that they are correct in this assessment. Secondly, let me note that in or around the 17th century Astrology ceased to be regarded as a science and was relegated to the category of pseudo-science. Again, I am strongly inclined to think that after this century it did indeed become a 'pseudo-science'. Thirdly, I note that (as far as I can determine) the reason astrology ceased to be a science was that scientists ceased to be interested in it: most likely, changes in fundamental ontology rendered astrological discourse irrelevant but more about this below. In one sense, I will argue, this is a perfectly valid reason for not regarding astrology as a science: science (so far as it is concerned with itself) is what scientists say it is and they have no reason to be interested in the things that don't interest them. Pseudo-sciences, I will propose below, are generally decomposition fragments of lost (or dormant) ontologies. Unlike philosophers or poets or psychologists scientists have no professional interest in alternative ontologies and this is a sufficient reason

---

[13]I checked after writing this sentence and lo and behold! http://skepticalsounds.blogspot.ca/2013/02/refuting-astrology.html. The authors claim that Astrology is un-falsifiable and empirically falsified not only in same article but in the very same paragraph!

(if you are a scientist) to dismiss them from the sphere of science. If you like, there is a public, objective natural realm accessible to the disciplines that fall under the umbrella of 'science' as that is understood, say, in a typical chemistry department. Anything else is of no interest or relevance as not fitting the values, paradigms and practices inscribed in the institutional structures of the sciences. So long as we are in the domain of science this is straightforward.

However, as cases like creationism and naturopathy prove this is not an idle question for the general public however much it might be a matter of indifference to practicing scientists. WE (the public that is) must decide at some point what is to count as knowledge and what is not and for this we would appear to need criteria of some sort. WE must have some mechanism for distinguishing science from pseudo-science or so it would appear. At some point we must decide, for instance, that astrology *will not* be a future program in the division of sciences or indeed in the arts (except as an object of purely historical inquiry). This is a *political* decision that must be made about an epistemic question and it cannot be made on quite the same grounds as a scientist would. We must have some way, beyond the question of *what* scientists do, of saying what *kind* of knowledge claims can be regarded as legitimate for the simple reason that we must distribute money and licenses to some practitioners and not others. Sometimes this kind of decision can be made on the basis of what is 'good science' and what is not but at other times it must be made on social or political grounds.

For instance, in a liberal state we cannot leave this kind of decision simply to the authority of one community (be it scientific or religious) but must recognize the claims of multiple constituencies: for example, the need to accommodate cultural diversity in the medical system may entail the licensing and use of traditional healing practices that are an uncomfortable fit with western scientific medicine. Also, allowance may need to be made for the anecdotal claims of fishermen or indigenous hunters. At the same time, we must be able to distinguish legitimate cultural diversity from exploitation and quackery. This means that we need not only some way to recognize legitimate and illegitimate science but also must distinguish both of these from 'cultural practices' which a multi-cultural society ought to tolerate.[14] Thus, we have a slightly more complex problem as citizens than we do as scientists.

---

[14] One of the problems here is our tendency to think that a 'culture' is a lens through which others peer while we gaze on reality directly. That science and indeed nature are things deeply embedded in the nexus of cultural signs is one of the themes of this book. From this standpoint it may become possible to recognize the claims of radically different cultures as manifesting rationality comparable to our own. As one indigenous scholar puts it: "Radical Indigenism dares to suggest, as its fundamental theoretical premise, that American Indian peoples possess philosophies of knowledge that can be understood as rationalities – articulable, coherent logics for ordering and knowing the world. This assumption permits us to understand these philosophies not merely as objects of curiosity (unusual things that people have believed) but as tools for discovery and for the generation of knowledge." (Garroute, Eva-Marie: "Defining "Radical Indigenism and Creating an American Indian Scholarship" in Pfohl, Stephan J. Culture, Power, and History: Studies in Critical Sociology.") 170.

After all, who is to say that the problem is not with the so-called pseudo-sciences but with the currently accepted ones? Is it actually a bad thing to have 'alternative' sciences which cannot be assimilated to our current world-view? Is it wrong to keep bits of ancient ontology fallow lest they should once again, in the future, blossom into something useful or interesting? Such considerations seem rather abstract perhaps, however, this demand can have considerable moral force when what is in question are, say, the ontologies and knowledge practices of indigenous peoples who are struggling to emerge from colonial domination. In this case a relational ontology sees human life as intimately, even pre-reflectively, connected to land and environment. This sentiment (if one can call it that) sometimes cuts across what archeology tells us of the pre-history of North America. Does this make the Hopi or the Innu of Labrador pseudo-scientific? Does it matter what archeology says about this? And what of Chinese or Indian systems of medicine? This raises the question of how the term 'pseudo-science' can be used to enforce various colonialisms and serve to entrench systems of privilege and domination. There may be many problems with acupuncture and homeopathy but one of them, historically at least, has been their implicit challenge to the status and power of orthodox physicians. Writers like Richard Dawkins not only defend western forms of reason but feel they need to pepper their comments with contemptuous jibes at indigenous cultures, using phrases like 'rain-dancing' and 'voodoo' as if they were self-evident terms of abuse. This is not accidental and should give us some pause about the less noble uses to which the idea of 'rationality' can be put.[15]

But wait, you might say, aren't you going to address the question of whether astrology is true? Isn't pseudo-science pseudo because it is false? Actually, I am not. Science can be false and still be science (i.e phlogiston or spontaneous generation). Conversely, pseudo-science can be true and still be pseudo-science: showing that parapsychology is not a legitimate science tells us nothing about the phenomena it investigates. Anyway, historically, I don't think the question of blunt empirical truth matters. There has never been, to my knowledge, a comprehensive scientific refutation of astrology (along the lines say of Weismann's supposed experimental refutation of Lamark).[16] Certainly, there wasn't one in the 17th century when

---

[15] An interesting account of this problem can be found in Cobern and Loving "Defining Science in a Multicultural World" (http://web.nmsu.edu/~ susanbro/educ451/docs/defining_science.pdf)

[16] One such experiment, involving simultaneous births, is recounted in great detail by St. Augustine (City of God V 1-7). Like many such experiments it sounds a bit too neat to be true. Though widely known as the work of a canonic author this passage did not impede the spread of Astrology in Medieval Europe, as Chaucer's Treatise on the Astrolabe, for example, attests. Versions of this 'twin test' have been performed in our day with discouraging results for Astrologers (http://www.telegraph.co.uk/news/uknews/1439101/Astrologers-fail-to-predict-proof-they-are-wrong.html) but if these studies do indeed refute astrology (a matter I am in no position to judge) that only makes it, by standard definitions, a science. Indeed, the critic of Astrology is here faced with a fork: if he touts supposed refutations of Astrology as definitive he has conceded that the claims of Astrologers are falsifiable and hence scientific. If, on the other hand, he concedes that the refutation in question

astrology ceased to be a science. There were arguments of course, there were sharp polemics of various kinds (often of a theological or philosophical nature) but no systematic empirical refutation for, if I am right about the nature of pseudoscience, none was ever required. Indeed, before the development of statistics no such refutation would even have been possible. For what it is worth however, I am just as happy to say that astrology was true in 1450 as to say that it is false now which, of course, entails the possibility that Astrology may one day become true again. But, you may also be wondering, aren't pseudo-sciences *bad* things? Maybe. Perhaps naturopaths and creationists ARE terrible people who do terrible things. I don't care at the moment. One of the advantages of the criterion I am seeking should be that it avoids moralism altogether. There need not be *any* undercurrent of imprecation or anathema to the use of the phrase pseudo-science that I am proposing.

To help you understand this, let me refer to a little article (now much anthologized) by a philosopher named Paul Thagard.[17] Thagard is concerned to show that Astrology is a pseudo-science. However, he argues that none of the standard arguments employed to show this really work: to his mind the sceptics like Carl Sagan, while justified in rejecting Astrology, have made a poor show of saying why. Thagard considers a number of standard objections to Astrology. Firstly, he considers the objection that Astrology is grounded in wishful thinking and magic and hence is not scientific. Thagard says that the first objection matters little to the truth or falsity of what Astrologers claim and the second ignores the origin of Chemistry in the dabbling of alchemists. (Thagard, 230) At any rate, these arguments claim far too much about the motivations of orthodox scientists: how many Chemistry experiments have their origin in the desire to bed a hot lab assistant or some other form of sexual or monetary wish fulfillment? Thagard then considers two further objections. First, he notes that one prominent critique of astrology objects to the fact that there is no known physical substrate that connects the planets and stars with the terrestrial events they supposedly influence. For Thagard this objection quickly comes to grief for the theory of continental drift was accepted long before its physical basis (plate tectonics) was understood. (230-31) Thagard might also have pointed to one glaring example of this phenomenon: the fact that natural selection became the standard theory in biology before its basis in genetics was understood.

---

is not definitive, that the Astrologer can still resort to ad hoc hypotheses, question the integrity of the researchers, dispute their methodology or even produce a contrasting study of his own then this again is no more than what scientists often do. We have by these means gotten no further towards showing that Astrology is a pseudo-science. At any rate, the key point is that Astrology became a 'pseudo-science' long before its supposed refutation. On the medieval reprisination of astrology as a probabilistic rather than a deterministic science see Kiekheffer (128-129).

[17] "Why Astrology is a Pseudo-Science" Proceedings of Philosophy of Science Association 1978, Vol.1. Cited from A Journey Through the Landscape of Philosophy ed. Jack Bowen (Pearson, 2008, New York). Thagard's treatment of this question seems to have attained canonical status.

18

Thagard then considers whether Astrology can be objected to on verificationist grounds. Are the claims of Astrologers empirically verifiable? This question, Thagard points out, scarcely matters. However verificationism and related doctrines may loom large in the public mind and shape the general perception of what science is they have little to no following whatsoever among philosophers, who rightly point out the verificationism has never been able to deal effectively with Hume's skeptical challenge to the idea of induction.(231)[18] Nor can it deal with the various self-referential paradoxes that the doctrine generates. What is more there are now crucial scientific theories, like string theory, which are at present amenable to no known technique of empirical testing. Further, even if verification did matter the claims of Astrologers are open to statistical tests such as those devised by French statistician Michel Gauquelin. (231) One cannot then, call Astrology a pseudo-science on the grounds that it is unverified or unverifiable.[19]

Well, perhaps we could say with Popper that the claims of Astrologers are so vague that they are in principle un-falsifiable? Alas, falsifiability as a demarcation principle is as dead in the water as verifiability. This may surprise some of you. Popper's principle has pervaded our discourse on science to such a degree that it has even attained the status of legal orthodoxy (in decisions involving the teaching of creation science). However, as Quine, Duhem and others have observed no theory that is sufficiently deep and comprehensive can be falsified by observation. (231) Nor should theories be falsified by observation. Newtonian physics was for many years falsified by the orbital path of the planet Mercury yet anyone with a brain could see that it was far too important a theory to throw over for the sake of a mere

---

[18] In an important sense there is no verification of our belief in the uniformity of nature or indeed of the generality of any scientific theory for uniformity and generality concern predictions about what will happen in the future whereas observation concerns only the now. Strictly speaking, verification can occur nowhere but in the immediate present and it was to address this problem (the so-called problem of induction) that the notion of falsification was introduced. It is precisely the 'law-like' universality that makes a proposition scientific which is incapable of verification! If it was in principle impossible to confirm a hypothesis because the process of verification extended indefinitely into the future it seemed more promising to say a theory could be falsified for falsifying observations need only occur in the present. However, for the reasons I will indicate the falsification principle proves notoriously difficult to apply.

[19] Standard accounts of hypothetico-deductive method (verifying hypotheses through observation) are highly problematic given that the formal statement of H/D, if p then q, but q therefore p commits the fallacy of affirming the consequent. Science thus carries on in defiance of basic logic. I leave it to the reader to decide whether this is a problem with science or a problem with logic. The case is not much better with falsification. The basic problem is this: if an observation falsifies a set of premises then either a. the fundamental theory is false b. some auxiliary hypotheses is false or c. some initial condition is false. However, no formalization of scientific method can say which of these three conditions obtains in a given instance leaving the scientist to muddle it out, perhaps abandoning his theory, perhaps modifying an auxiliary hypothesis etc. He is, however, never forced by observation to do the former rather than the latter. An example of this is the much bruited problem of replication. Failure to replicate an experiment can be taken as a falsification but just as easily as an equipment failure or lack of 'know-how' on the part of the replicator.

empirical hiccup. Thus, Astrology is as falsifiable or un-falsifiable as any other basic scientific theory. Thus, Thagard finds that falsification cannot be used to demarcate Astrology from the other legitimate sciences.

By no means does Thagard consider Astrology to be a real science. All of this skepticism is merely an appetizer to the main course. Thagard has his own solution to the demarcation problem which he thinks entirely adequate to deal with the claims of pseudo-scientists such as Astrologers. I say this with the proviso that his demarcation criteria are nuanced and contextual. They do not determine what is a pseudo-science for all times and all places. Thus, Thagard admits that for much of its history Astrology was a science. His claim, however, is that it is not one now. This, of course, entails that it could become one in the future but Thagard does not seem greatly bothered by this. His claim is basically this: the problem with astrology is not so much what it says as how its practitioners behave. True scientists, Thagard says, are progressives. Astrologers, on the other hand, are reactionaries. The distinction between science and pseudo-science is a social and institutional one not a logical or methodological one. Here is what he says: "A theory or discipline which purports to be scientific is pseudo-scientific if and only if 1. It has been less progressive than alternative theories over a long period of time, and faces many unsolved problems; but 2. The community of practitioners makes little attempt to develop the theory towards solutions of the problems, shows no concern for attempts to evaluate the theory in relation to others, and is selective in considering confirmations and disconfirmations." (p. 233). Thus, scientists are people who 'behave' one way and pseudo-scientists are people who 'behave' another way and science can be understood, one supposes, in behavioral or operational terms.[20]

Let me leave aside the question of confirmations and disconfirmations which, as we have seen, is somewhat vexed. The first bit is more interesting. It is not a problem for Thagard if astrologers have not solved problems like the precession of the equinoxes or the differences between the personalities of twins. It is precisely such problems that underlie the development of research programs. (232) Nor does it matter that Astrologers disagree about the significance of new planets (or dwarf planets) such as Pluto or Eris. Presumably we *want* scientists to have doubts and disagreements. No, the *real* problem Thagard tells us lies in the excessive pragmatism and hence excessive conservatism of Astrologers. Astrologers tend to eschew theoretical reflection and confine their practice to the drawing of horoscopes (shut up and do the math!). Because of this basic problems in the discipline have remained unaddressed for centuries. Moreover, competing theories such as psychoanalysis have arisen which address the same domain as Astrologers do[21]. Yet the astrological community continues as before making no at-

---

[20]Of course in some ways Astrologers behave exactly like scientists: they speak in a complex professional jargon for instance. It appears then that we require an account of which behaviors are essential to scientists which can scarcely be done in behavioral terms for which behaviors do we regard as relevant to the question and why?

[21]A somewhat ironic example on Thagard's part given the interest of Jung and his

tempt to take account of these new theories and not developing their own to take account of them. (233) In all this they show themselves to be unthinking pragmatists rather than true scientists: they are practitioners of an art but are not reflective about that art. Astrology is pseudo-science because it is fossilized science. Consider then the following statement: "What makes astrology pseudo-scientific is not that it lacks periods of Kuhnian normal science, but that its proponents adopt the uncritical attitudes of "normal" scientists despite the existence of more progressive alternative theories." (p. 233) It seems, then, that a pseudoscience is only possible under *certain definite historical conditions* and that in the 12th century, say, Astrology could not have been a pseudo-science had it tried! Indeed, as contingencies of life and personality are deeply puzzling and Astrology was one way of understanding these it may have claimed (in a pre-psychological age) to be the worst theory going except for all the others.

Of course, this has nothing to do directly with the actual content of Astrology or any of the other pseudo-sciences mentioned above. Would Thagard say that the content of creation science would be scientific if, under altered circumstances, it would begin to show traits of progressiveness?[22] What if homeopaths began to take account of other medical theories and altered their practices and theories accordingly? This is an intriguing question for, in the 17th century, Astrology was beginning to show some sign of a progressive discipline with Kepler, for instance, proposing radical revisions to the traditional system of houses and Zodiacal signs.[23] Yet this was just the period when Astrology ceased to be considered a science. Why would Astrology begin its long decline just at the point where, by Thagard's definition, it was becoming an actual science? Thagard seems aware of the problem and this is why he continues thus: "The simple answer is that a theory can take on the appearance of an unpromising project well before it deserves the label of pseudo-science. The Copernican revolution and the mechanism of Newton, Descartes and Hobbes undermined the plausibility of Astrology." (p. 234) How did the aforementioned phenomena do this? Thagard continues: " . . . .Newtonian theory pushed aside what had been

---

followers in astrological charts. (see Rossi and Le Grice Jung on Astrology, 1-2) For Jung, horoscopes were a form in which archetypal powers of the psyche externalized themselves by introjection into the constellations and planets. This essentially psychological account of astrology seems, whatever one thinks of it, just the kind of revision of the discipline Thagard says is essential to progressive science. This is because Jung has put the practice of drawing horoscopes on an entirely new ontological footing: when we meditate the stars we read only ourselves in them. This is why a contemporary practitioner such as Richard Tarnas can speak of 'archetypal astrology' though he goes rather farther than Jung asserting an ". . . intrinsic aesthetic splendor in the universe, an overflow of cosmic intelligence and delight that reveals itself in this continuous marriage of mathematical astronomy and mythic poetry." (http://gaiamind.org/AstroIntro.html)

[22]It is one of the oddities of Popper's falsification theory that crackpot theories seem to become scientific the instant they are discredited. Thagard's theory seems to me open to comparable objections: Creation Science did indeed progress (in Thagard's sense) when its proponents revised their thesis into the intelligent design hypothesis which, whatever one thinks of it, certainly differs (formally) from young earth creationism.

[23]See "Kepler's Belief in Astrology" in History and Astrology (Unwin Paperbacks, London, 1989) 164-66.

accepted as a universal natural law, that inferiors such as inhabitants of the earth are ruled and governed by superiors such as the stars and planets." (p. 234) This is interesting. It seems that Thagard's account of pseudo-science is not a comfortable fit with the history as he himself recounts it. The decline of Astrology seems to have little to do with its status as a non-progressive research program. Rather, Thagard hints at a fundamental change in ontology from a hierarchal to a mechanist conception. This notion will take some unpacking, which I will do in the next section. Let me just note for now that research programs become stagnant precisely because they are suspect for some other reason. Theories and disciplines die *when* they stop getting grants and stop progressing not *because* they stop getting grants and stop progressing. Work on them stops when they become uninteresting or unpromising for *other* reasons. In other words, their *content* becomes unappealing, not their form. Thus, we may, after all, need the notion of content to get at our intuition about what is wrong with homeopathy or the other 'excluded' disciplines. Indeed, following Thagard's hint here we may see our way to formulating what is pseudo in a pseudo-science.

To further clarify this problem let me say a few words about astrology. Firstly, what is it that Astrologers assert? Broadly speaking they claim, of course, that the stars and planets influence the course of terrestrial events and shape our lives and character. Astrologers claim to chart these influences by a traditional system of 'houses and signs' and by noting the relative positions or 'aspects' of various planets at the time of one's birth. Thus, if Mars and Venus are in opposition to one another one would expect to find in one's personality a 'clash' of some sort between these archetypal patterns of personality (as with Chaucer's Wife of Bath!). For what it's worth, I am sure I am not alone in finding the results of this process, which can be carried to great lengths of complexity, a roughly adequate sketch of my own personality. I think this fact is worth noting whatever one thinks of Astrology as a science or of the stars as causes: whether they were scientists or not I suppose the creators of Astrology to have been at very least shrewd and to have included a considerable amount of data on their human subjects within their charts. It is for this reason I suppose that astrology is a hobby or passion, perhaps even a useful tool for self-discernment for all kinds of people who have no particular beliefs about the structure of the cosmos.[24] Of course Astrologers have also claimed to answer other kinds

---

[24]Insofar as Astrology, of its very nature, includes much information on patterns of character and indeed may be said to lay out a system of personal archetypes it may well be (pace Thagard) as reasonable to resort to it as to more reputable bodies of knowledge such as Jungian or Freudian analysis which are (like Astrology itself) as personally illuminating as they are scientifically problematic. To its devotees it has heuristic value apart from whether it is a literal representation of the world. In this it resembles nothing so much as models, metaphors or other heuristic tools such as may be found in many of the sciences. Even the ancients knew that aspects of the astrological chart had no actual correspondence to the physical heavens (Luck, Arcana Mundi, 380). This matters only if you think it is the job of a theory to correspond to external facts. An instrumentalist interpretation of Astrology which finds it a useful

of questions: questions involving the influences under which a work should be begun or concluded, questions involving the mundane affairs of daily life etc. This latter sort of Astrology is called horary astrology as opposed to 'natal' Astrology which is concerned with character or the study of 'transits' which concern personal crises or upheavals.

There is much in this that may puzzle us at first glance. I admit to some puzzlement myself as to how the symbolic and mathematical aspects of this 'science' go together: in fact, this seems to me a basic incoherence.[25] Of course, quantum mechanics and evolutionary theory puzzle me too. I have no idea how a sequence of chemicals can encode such seemingly rarified character traits as sexual preference. My puzzlement says nothing about the success or failure of population genetics or quantum mechanics as mathematical formalisms. Moreover Astrology does rest on a very sophisticated conception. In fact, it is in some respects the neo-Platonic science par excellence.[26] As far as I can see, it rests on a two basic principles which are, ultimately, Platonic in character. The first is the principle of hierarchy. The universe exists in a gradated scale of causes and powers from the highest and most universal to the most local and restricted. The sun works everywhere on earth but my computer works in my house. Agency, in this scheme, is *descending* from the most generic to the most specific. Thus, the heavenly bodies as the highest entities (i.e. the most lasting, most powerful and best) have the broadest scope as causes and are, as it were, the first principle of movement for the cosmic chain. The second principle is that of sympathy or correspondence. This is a bit tricky to get at but perhaps I can put it like this: the ancient ontology of the Platonists was prepared (as ours is not) to allow symbolic (or more properly analogical) associations to function as principles or laws. Thus, apparently symbolic correspondences functioned as real links between macrocosmic whole and microcosmic part. This was an accepted part of ontology. Grant these two

---

calculating tool would not have to worry over much about such problems as the procession of the equinoxes, the fact that the constellations no longer align with the traditional signs of the Zodiac. Attempts to address this deficiency by Claudius Ptolemy met with little interest perhaps indicating that the question was not vexing to ancient practitioners. (Lawrence, Hellenistic Astrology, 29)

[25] There seems no intrinsic logical principle binding the symbolism of the zodiac with the position and movement of the planets. Of course condemning Astrology on these grounds would assume that no 'legitimate' science suffers this sort of defect: i.e. a split between mathematical form and representative content.

[26] Most of the ancient Platonists and Platonizing Stoics accepted astrology in some form or other though, some, such as Plotinus, expressed skepticism about the practice of drawing personal horoscopes. (Luck, 427) In general they accepted the stars as signs in which we could read divine fate though they divided on the question of whether the stars were active agents in transmitting this fate. Plotinus was very hesitant to attribute evil to the stars and always held that the soul transcended fate. His pupil Porphyry however was much more open to the claims of astrologers (Lawrence, 35-37) It is worth pointing out though that everyone in Antiquity and indeed everyone today accepts what for Astrologers was a first principle i.e. that celestial events affect terrestrial ones as is evident from such phenomena as the seasons and the tides. Indeed, as the science which unfolded the unity of heaven and earth Astrology fulfilled a basic theoretical and spiritual function, a desideratum expressed eloquently by Boethius at the conclusion of the second book of his Consolation of Philosophy.

points together and Astrology becomes a promising hypothesis for we have both a causal principle and a manifest link between that causal principle and terrestrial events. The sidereal becomes something in which we can *read* the terrestrial. The stars *predict* what they *symbolize* by their aspects. Thus, we are told (by Sir Phillip Sidney no less!) that: "Though dusty wits dare scorn Astrology... for me I do Nature unidle know, and know great causes, great effects procure: and know those bodies high reign on the low." (Sidney,1982; *Astrophel and Stella* Sonnet XXVI)

It is perhaps impossible for us to sense how easy and inevitable this inference could be for many of the ancients. In a symbolic ontology founded on the notion of gradation and hierarchy where else would we look for ultimate causes but to the stars?[27] Of course there has long been one major challenge to astrology and it comes from ethics and theology and not from science: I refer, of course, to Christian and Jewish notions of free will and human responsibility which sort oddly with astral determinism. St. Augustine, for instance, was notorious for his polemics against astrology and he was not without followers on this subject even in the high Renaissance. Thus, Christian theology was, for much of its existence, a significant source of opposition to the practice of astrology. Of course, it was always open to the Christian astrologer to conceive his discipline in what we would now call probabilistic terms. He could argue that the stars were a causal influence without being an absolutely determinative influence. Plotinus seems to endorse this point of view, holding the stars to be a real influence but not one that can overcome our free will. (Luck, 2006; 424) This, however, was not enough to save astrology from historical eclipse. This is because a radical revision of ontology rendered the hierarchical and symbolic conceptions of astrology untenable. The new *Christian* science of the early modern period reduced all causes to a plane of equality and subordinated all nature equally to the will of God. Thus, the antique doctrines of causal hierarchy, which co-existed with Christianity in the middle ages, were flattened and eliminated by a new emphasis on the absolute power of god and the inertness of matter: Descartes' infinite substance and his passive *res extensa*. In this context, what had seemed an inevitable inference for many of the ancients became an absurd superstition. Moreover, the doctrines of sympathy and correspondence became an arch absurdity as quantity became the reigning principle and qualitative relationships were dismissed as occult. Together these two conceptions sealed the fate of the astrologers and their practice

---

[27]I should point out here that we in the contemporary west do allow that factors such genetics or chemicals in the uterine environment can influence the development of personality and have some predictive value. This is not a belief that differs fundamentally from that of astrologers who hold the same view but assign our behavior a different cause. For them this was because (like our fetishizing of the gene perhaps) the stars were physical determinants par excellence. It is also interesting to note that the very same debates over determinism and free will swirl around genetics. However, the crucial point is that a chain or a ladder was the constitutive metaphor of ancient science where ours is perhaps still the machine. One cannot really discover anything about nature without such metaphors yet the metaphor you choose determines much of what you subsequently observe.

died with a whimper rather than a bang.

Is there a lesson here? I think there is. The first is that theories about pseudo-science have little relation to how, historically, the realm of legitimate science is demarcated or how it is demarcated today. In the instance we have looked at, the range of possible sciences has been demarcated by theological, metaphysical and ethical considerations: by factors that are *extra-scientific*. The relation of pseudo-science to science seems to be that the former includes elements of superseded ontologies which have no systematic 'fit' with current conceptions. This explains the precipitous intellectual decline that sets in once something has been banished to the pseudo-scientific realm. A discipline like astrology no longer attracts a Kepler or a Ptolemy and retrenches itself as a practice with little or no theoretical reflection. It survives like a vestigial trait in an organism. It seems clear to me then that the 'pseudo' of pseudo-science is at least in part contextual as alternative 'sciences' often have non-standard metaphysical conceptions at their base. Given that any science at all has some 'metaphysic' or other encoded in it we might well ask whether, at least in some cases, pseudo-science may be more *otherly* rational than irrational.

Perhaps though, you feel I have missed something vital. Surely the problem with all of these spurious disciplines is one of evidence! Homeopaths surely believe in something that has not a scrap of evidence to support it. Actually, Homeopathy has a great deal of evidence to support it: all the evidence to which homeopaths point! But, you will say, this is not *good* evidence or *strong* evidence. Much of it, for instance, is anecdotal. Perhaps you are right but, without writing another paper on another difficult topic (what is *good* about good evidence? Is a purple fish good evidence that crows are black?)[28] I will content myself with the following remarks: one of the things that makes evidence *bad* is lack of fit with other evidence that we accept as valid. Evidence of human footprints from the Jurassic would involve overturning so much accepted knowledge and accepted theory that it would be more parsimonious to regard it as an unexplained anomaly or a forgery. We are not convinced by evidence that does not 'fit' with current knowledge no matter how strong it may appear *prima facie*.

Probably we are right to be conservative in this sense for the universe is not piecemeal where knowledge is concerned. I recall reading somewhere that an observer on the English coast was once able to accurately describe a ship that should have been invisible on present knowledge of the curvature of the earth. Apocryphal or not this tale will not turn anyone into a flat-earther nor should it. At least ordinarily: the question of scientific revolutions (whose empirical evidence must seem anomalous to the reigning paradigm in just this way) comes up here but that again would be another paper! Suffice it to say that considerable judgment is needed to see when

---

[28] If I assert "all crows are black" the contrapositive of this "all non-black things are non-crows" follows logically. This means that the first proposition could be verified by instances of the second though it seems paradoxical to say that purple fish or blue stars are evidence that crows are black. This problem was first proposed by Carl Hempel. It has remained controversial since.

this criterion of consistency with current theories and knowledge needs to be suspended to allow for revolutionary transformations. Nonetheless it is often the case that persisting in a style of rationality or form of life other than the one you inhabit may indeed be grounded in pathological stubbornness: holocaust deniers might be taken as pertinent examples of this. If everything they claim turned out to be true we would still regard them (rightly) as cranks because their intellectual motivations and their research procedures are perverse.

Perhaps then in despite of my desire to avoid moralism I have come round to an ethical consideration after all. A pseudo-scientist may at the end of the day be someone who is conducting a dialogue of the deaf. Let me explain: *after* the collapse of the hierarchical 'layer cake' ontology that undergirded the science of Astrology one has two choices: one can a. become a metaphysician and seek to restore the old ontology to its previous status or b. one may continue on as if nothing has happened. In neither case is one a scientist or a practitioner of a science. This is because one is engaged in a project *prior* to science or one is not inquiring or questioning at all (and questioning is one thing I take to be essential to the scientific stance). The astrologer must engage in thinking that is either above or beneath scientific thinking. As such, he is not and cannot be a participant in the discourse of science. He or she must be an intellectual adventurer of an unusual sort (and there is nothing wrong with that) or indeed one of the blunt, incurious people Thagard thinks astrologers have become.[29] Most crucially the latter person is carrying on a practice without reflecting on the ontology that underlies it or even holding one contrary to it. Because of this he shows a fundamental incapacity for dialogue or development: his views stagnate because they are held in an arbitrary and purely external manner. To this extent he has many of the traits we would attribute to a pseudo-scientist.

For now let this stand as my two cents worth on the nature of pseudo-science: to some degree we have confirmed Paul Thagard's intuition that it is the attitudes and practices of astrologers that make them pseudo-scientists more so than the content of their assertions. We have added the proviso however that the stubbornness of the pseudo-scientist is in the service of an ontology which is superseded and may be inconsistent with many of the pseudo-scientist's own ordinary conceptions. There are cultural environments, such as Tibetan monasteries or Sufi orders, where the phenomenon we label as 'ESP' are readily accepted as consistent with current ontologies. There are other environments, such as Biology departments, where they are not readily accepted because they are *inconsistent* with

---

[29] A metaphysical adventurer may not be uncalled for. At the base of the problems we are looking at here lies the unfortunate fact that our reigning philosophy, empiricism, is an awkward fit for our sciences as Kant long ago realized. If one begins, as the Cartesians did, with a reduction of causality to efficient and material causes it may be hard to escape the skepticism of Hume and all the repercussions it has had in 20th Century philosophy of science. It is interesting to note then that formal causality at least may be coming, as all fundamental things do at some point, back into vogue. (https://www.firstthings.com/article/2018/08/aristotle-returns)

current ontologies. This is not a problem: people have every right to their ontologies.[30] We may legitimately wonder though whether a person who engages in such extreme compartmentalization as to mix beliefs that entail one ontology with beliefs that entail another is being sufficiently reflective. Creationists may well be instances of such people.

Sadly, this does not solve every problem. We are still left with the fact that what from one perspective may be viewed as pseudo-science might be viewed as revolutionary science from another. As Paul Feyerabend has argued the situation of revolutionary science is, in its initial phases, scarcely different from that of pseudo-science. For instance, Heliocentrism violated what to previous centuries had been a sound methodological principle: that science assumes the natural viewpoint of the observer and orders the appearances accordingly. In reviving the theory of the ancient Pythagoreans it also revived an archaic and superseded theory that had been abundantly falsified by observation (i.e. the fact that we are not hurled off our swiftly moving planet). Galileo however engaged in a comprehensive re-description of these same facts in terms of a new kind of relativistic physics. A different theoretical framework resulted in new set of facts and a different description of the old facts (such as the fact that a stone dropped from a tower falls at its base). As Feyerabend points out, Galileo proceeded *against* the facts and against empirical method to produce a radical revolution in scientific thinking (1988,14). Early modern astronomy, then, seems to violate even the modest criteria I have set out in this paper. The criteria allow us to say why some things might be considered pseudo-science in some contexts and from some points of view but no more. They cannot of their

---

[30]Of course at this point some may attempt to make the argument that we reject ESP and cognate phenomenon not because of our underlying ontology but because 'extraordinary claims require extraordinary evidence'. However, the claim that a phenomenon is 'extraordinary' seems to me a signal instance of a judgment that depends on ontology, on what you are predisposed to think is 'ordinary' or not. I suppose levitation to be no great deal in Tibetan monasteries. One might say that this is because Tibetan monks are prone to hallucination. One might also say that belief in levitation is caused by levitation. Which one prefers is a function of one's metaphysics. Our metaphysic, naturalism, has certain stock responses to anomalous events like levitation: hallucination and fraud being most prominent. I assume Buddhist ontology has stock responses for events that are anomalous to it. These stock responses allow us to retain our ontologies in spite of apparent falsifications. As a perfect illustration of this consider the work of para-psychology researcher Daryl Bem. Bem has shown in rigorous experiments that the phenomenon of precognition is real. Do psychologists now accept the phenomenon? Of course they don't. Bem's research has lead not to a revision of the standard views on pre-cognition but to a reconsideration of experimental method in psychology. As Daniel Egber puts it, if E.S.P is real then science is broken! Why is he so certain of this? He suggests in one place that E.S.P violates logic though he gives no logical principle it violates (Modus ponens? Excluded middle?). His actual objection is an a priori metaphysical principle: time is unidirectional! Thus, anything that falsifies this fundamental principle of ontology must be mistaken and if by current methods we cannot locate this mistake then it is our reigning methodologies we must reconsider. With apologies to Popper it is clear from this that an apriori metaphysical principle cannot be falsified by any empirical event, even one as commonly experienced by ordinary people as pre-cognition. (http://redux.slate.com/cover-stories/2017/05/daryl-bem-proved-esp-is-real-showed-science-is-broken.html)

nature be universally prescriptive. Perhaps this means I have failed in the task I set myself. Perhaps we really are left with Larry Laudan's suggestion that we should not worry about whether our beliefs are scientific (or pseudo-scientific) so much as whether our beliefs are, in some broader sense, warranted. This may involve abandoning the belief that scientific procedures involve some *special and privileged kind of warrant*. (1983; 111-127) In Laudan's view many of the beliefs of football coaches or carpenters have more warrant than the beliefs of string theorists or exo-biologists. Other beliefs might have much less warrant than competing scientific notions. Of course, Aristotle tells us that science surpasses craft knowledge by knowing the *why* of things, the knowledge of causes. (*Metaphysics* 981a, 30) However we must sometimes face the sober truth that, with a view to action at least: "... experience seems in no respect inferior to art, and men of experience succeed even better than those who have theory without experience." (981a, 15) Falsity, it seems, can have the form of science while truth can have the form of craft-knowledge! However, a fuller discussion of warrant and its relationship to the various domains of knowledge is for another day.

3 WEIRD SCIENCE

If I were to give this essay a clumsier title I would call it 'weird beliefs about science'. My claim is that some of the things people believe about the activity we call science are probably, nay, almost certainly weird. The first is that the sciences (we should in fact pluralize this word) are an instrument for uncovering 'facts'. Facts are things that exist independently of minds. One of the things suggested by the most sophisticated science of our time, Quantum Mechanics, is that mind is a constitutive principle of the observed world: subject and object together constitute the world. Science itself suggests that the 'realism' and 'objectivism' that most defenders of science presume is its core message may be no message at all. Of course to philosophers this is old hat: it was Socrates himself who first suggested millennia ago that any inquiry into nature had to begin with knowledge of ourselves: hence his turn from natural science to the study of ethical concepts. (Aristotle, *Metaphysics* I, 987 b) Later, Plotinus informed us that before we claimed any knowledge of the world we had first to investigate the mind knowing it. (*Enneads* V,1) Famously, this issued (in modernity) in the 'critical turn' of Kant, who examined the a priori categories that structure our experience in his magisterial *Critique of Pure Reason*. However, science in our time has also come around to seeing the observer as an essential part of the phenomenon observed and indeed as constituting (rather than simply observing) events in the sub-atomic world. The other weird belief is that the 'objective fact world' is related to science as an object to its mirror. Neither of these things strike me as plausible and I will proceed to show why.

First let's make a distinction. Questions about science are not scientific questions. Science investigates nature, that is its domain. It does not investigate itself. Yet we speak about science all the time often with a capital S. If I say 'science is the truth' or 'science is all bunk' I have made a global assertion about it grounded not in scientific evidence (how can it be?) but some other kind. Well, what sort of evidence do we have about science? One way (not the only way) to inquire into science is to study it as a set of practices in an institutional setting. How is our knowledge of the world shaped by the fact that science is embedded in the world of politics, economics and so on? Broadly, such an investigation would use not experimental reasoning but the descriptive/interpretive methods of the social sciences.[31] Thus, we can speak of a 'sociology' of knowledge. Here is a simple example. Any scientist works with a budget. What we get from her is not the truth per se but the truth as filtered through, say, a $ 10,000 spending limit. Thus, if we ask ourselves about a certain fact concerning the planet Pluto our answer is partly determined by what is happening on Pluto and partly determined by the nature of our equipment.[32] If our scientist has $ 10,000 dollars the temperature of Pluto will be one thing. If she has $ 100,000 dollars to spend the temperature on Pluto, will, presumably, be something much more exact. The 'fact' is in fact an 'artifact' that is simultaneously the product of natural conditions and of social or political conditions (like the budget of NASA). Nature + budget=equals scientific truth! This is as much as to say that every natural event we observe is simultaneously a constructed event. Of course if I write V=D/T there is no way for me to factor B (budget) into the equation. The social constitution of a scientific fact is occluded by science itself not as an accident or an error but as something intrinsic to the scientific enterprise.[33] Of course, different

---

[31]This kind of work has been carried out by scholars such a Bruno Latour and the members of the so-called Edinburgh School. Such scholars have produced a kind of social history of the sciences as a supplement to the usual 'whig' accounts of science which see it simply in the terms of the supposedly inevitable triumph of truth over ignorance and superstition. With broader institutional or cultural factors in mind one might, for instance, see in the triumph of the heliocentric model more than a simple triumph of truth over falsity (though it may in part be that). One may see it as expressing broader cultural trends like the re-evaluation in the Renaissance of the importance of the Pythagorean/Platonic tradition in philosophy and the consequent pull towards symbols and ideas that valorize the sun (Plato's sensible analogue of the 'Good'). Of course, whether or not this implies 'radical relativism' is a subject of much debate. The present writer commends not so much relativism as hermeneutic caution and a healthy respect for difference.

[32]A fact adverted to by Hegel over two centuries ago: "For if knowledge is the instrument by which to get possession of absolute reality, the suggestion immediately occurs that the application of an instrument to anything does not leave it as it is in itself but entails in the process, and has in view, a moulding or alteration of it." (Phenomenology of Mind, 131).

[33]Consider the question of testing intelligence which Shermer adverts to on page 47. How smart, say, is Mr. Smith? Can we quantify his intelligence? Well, Mr. Smith in the course of his day may have to perform a multitude of tasks. He may have to analyze a poem, solve a quadratic equation, negotiate with his boss, talk to his kids about drugs, plane some boards or make decisions about his finances. All of these require intelligence of some kind. But is there one general function 'g' measured by 'IQ' that allows him to do all these things? Well that seems doubtful on its face as people's abilities to perform these tasks vary considerably. Some people will do the equation well and fail dismally at talking to their kids and vice versa. So 'intelligence' at least seems to be a collection of a number of specified functions. For the sake of argument though let me grant that Mr. Smith is 'intelligent' in some broader sense than 'good at this' or 'good at that'. Now if we wanted to measure this general intelligence we will have to devise a test of some kind but what things shall we test for? Out of the hundreds of things we do we have to single out a set of tasks which will reveal this general intelligence, like rotating triangles in our heads or solving verbal puzzles, as opposed to writing limericks or sestinas. But on what principle shall we make this determination? Here is where the biases of the researcher play not an accidental role but a NECESSARY one: values will inevitably be a part of how intelligence is measured. In a technocratic society our test will be heavily weighted towards problem solving and abstract reasoning as opposed to story-telling or singing. Measuring instruments CONSTRUCT the object measured as much as they reflect it.

societies agree on all kinds of things like avoiding fire or respecting courage over cowardice. Still, if we took all the things upon which humans agreed we would have not reality but the scaffolding on which it is built. It takes culture to determine nature to a specific form and science is one of the ways this is done.

Thus we can see in a very simple way how the condition of the subject is a necessary moment in the mediation of the object. The instrument used to measure the temperature of Pluto has to cost something and what it costs will be an essential component of the facts uncovered. There is reality and the filters through which we view it and we do not get the first absent the second. This is obvious in the case of instruments which depend on things like the state of machine tooling or the degree of industrial development in a given society.[34] The social constitution of knowledge however takes many other forms. One is authority. Professor Smith is the world's leading authority on widgets but he is not only this. At the same time, he sits on the editorial boards of key journals and is frequently consulted by granting agencies. If the field of widgetology is a small one the odds are great that most of the papers written on it will be sent to professor Smith to review. Moreover, the fact that professor Smith has taught many students who carry on his research methods and reflexively support his conclusions further extends his power. The conclusion is obvious: the truth about widgets will be whatever professor Smith says it is. He or his students will be highly unlikely to give grants to researchers whose methods do not match his own. Papers that argue conclusions contrary to his own will be declined or sent back to be revised into something more to his liking. Young researchers will quickly figure out that if they want publications in high impact journals (something essential for their careers) they would be fools to cross professor Smith. This kind of gatekeeping is deplorable but also essential. Science journals cannot publish just anything: determinations must be made and the personal authority of scientists, their biases and interests will be part and parcel of this process. Knowledge is filtered through authority structures as much as through instruments and changes in both entail changes in the world we inhabit.

The situation is only more complex when we factor in corporate, military or political interests. These determine what we know about nature by

---

So, we devise our test and create a statistical artifact: 'IQ'. If we are honest researchers, we will admit that this artifact at best indirectly reflects at least some (though surely not all) of our real life abilities. Alas this is not what the popular belief in IQ entails. The popular version takes this statistical artifact and makes of it a thing that actually exists in peoples' heads though these in fact contain neurons and synapses not mythical beasts like IQ's. Moreover, people do this because they see IQ as a mechanism by which social privileges can be granted or denied and here is where the inevitable political/social dimension (IQ tests for geometric or spatial reasoning over bread baking or the art of the deal) becomes nasty politics. This is as much as to say that science is as bound by the hermeneutic circle as any other form of interpretation.

[34] A striking example of this is the heliocentric theory which could not be confirmed empirically until there were telescopes able to observe the stellar parallax. The fact that helio-centrism became the dominant model in astronomy long before this suggests that we over-rate empirical confirmation.

determining what kind of research is funded. To a shocking degree they also retain a veto over results.[35] Any scientist who goes against the corporate interests that fund her lab knows she is in for a long, expensive fight. This is a fight the corporation involved does not even need to win. All they need do is make it protracted and personally grueling. At any rate one does not even need to appeal to the fact that corporations resort to threats, bribery and corruption as these imply the problem would go away if only people were good. This is not the case. Not every domain of nature can be investigated. Priorities have to be established. Some of these will be established by the curiosity of scientists but not all. Some will be the product of wars and the need to develop new weaponry. Others will be established by donors whether these be government officials or CEO's. Even if all of these players were honest and above board the fundamental fact would remain: many questions go unasked and many domains of nature go un-researched. For every theory that is developed there will be others that are neglected. Data that for all we know could be crucial or telling for our current world view will remain uncollected. In other words, we cannot investigate all of the natural world, in fact, we cannot investigate more than a sliver of it. Answers depend upon the questions asked and the questions asked depend upon the interests of the questioner. These can be professional, personal, economic, military or political. Thus, nature is not only filtered through instruments or through the personal biases of authority figures. It is filtered through the needs of the institutions that fund scientific research. We get as much insight into nature as these limiting conditions allow.[36]

There is some truth then to the assertion of Marx that things like science (and other forms of culture like philosophy or religion) rest on an institutional base. Change that institutional base in some crucial way and scientific knowledge will change along with it. New instruments, new authority structures and new institutional priorities will produce a new nature

---

[35]Particularly grotesque was the treatment of Dr. Nancy Olivieri by the drug company Apotex. (https://umanitoba.ca/faculties/arts/departments/philosophy/ethics/media/Drug_Trial.pdf) In spite of determinations by the Canadian Association of University Teachers that her academic freedom was violated Dr. Olivieri was still the subject of attacks years after the fact. On the general problem of corporate malfeasance in medical research see the Union of Concerned Scientists, Citizens and Scientists for Environmental Studies. "Heads They Win Tails We Lose: How Corporations Corrupt Science at the Public's Expense" (2012)

[36]Mr. Shermer is honest and informed enough to recognize this fact (46-48). The difference between us is that while he thinks theory-ladeness, observer bias and so on are problems with science (problems, presumably, which due diligence can overcome) I follow Gadamer in thinking that they are, in fact, conditions of the possibility of science. Bias is present in the very constitution of a science which means, of course, that it loses some of its pejorative connotations. This, if you like, is the hermeneutic revolution. That said there are biases which are, to put it mildly, less than foundational and we should of course strive to remove these, however much this might be a counsel of perfection. At any rate Nietzsche is, as usual, apt on this point: "Strictly speaking there is no such thing as science "without any pre-suppositions" ; this thought does not bear thinking through, it is paralogical: a philosophy, a "faith" , must always be there first of all, so that science can acquire from it a direction, a meaning, a limit, a method, a right to exist." (The Gay Science 5, 344)

for us to inhabit, one that perhaps has many points of contact with the old one but is novel in ways that cannot readily be foreseen. The reason for this is the structural one I have here laid out: truth is a meeting of subject and object.[37] The thing known is in the knower according to the mode of the knower. The conditions the subject brings to the natural world (and every subject brings some) co-operate with nature to produce the realm of fact: our social world and the natural world are co-relatives. This is just a determination of a broader fact: that our minds and the world together produce the truth. "The eye altering alters all" says William Blake. (*The Mental Traveler*, 1978;501) This is true on the practical social level as Marx held and as we have seen in this brief essay. Kant may well be correct that it is true on a deeper a priori as well (except that for Kant these categories are not historical i.e. they do not alter). Be that as it may I think I have established that science is not a straight transcription of a world of objective fact. It is not a pure mirror but a heavily tinted one. It brings as much to the natural world as it takes from it and this is why it is subject to revolutions and profound transformations from one historical epoch to the next.

---

[37]Consider the following case. Mr. Wade Davis tells us in his Haiti travelogue The Serpent and the Rainbow that at the basis of the 'zombie' phenomenon lies tetrodotoxin, the venom of the puffer fish. I'm no toxicologist but let us assume for the moment that he is correct. In Japan there are a certain range of effects that follow from tetrodotoxin poisoning. These same effects exist in Haiti along with a whole new chain of effects that can render its victims catatonic for years at a time. In each case the physical properties of the puffer toxin operate within a cultural script that uses the physical fact as its basis. In each script the chemical, while retaining some of its base properties, operates in wholly new ways to produce a range of different effects. It is never a fact without being an artifact. (see Davis, 130) To put it bluntly, a chemical reaction is at the same time a cultural event.

4 LIGHT BELIEFS: ON FAIRIES AND PHILOSOPHY

One of the things that seems to be assumed in any discussion of belief is that beliefs are serious things. This is because they often are serious things. I however have many unserious beliefs: these include things like lake monsters. I don't seriously believe in lake monsters. Not a single action of mine is predicated on the existence of such an entity. Nor do I trouble to defend their existence to anyone. I suppose all I really do is refrain from strenuously attacking people who do have serious beliefs about Nessie, Ogopogo and the like. This is a belief I wear lightly because light belief seems to me what it warrants. If I may be so quaint, it seems to me that light beliefs are something a gentleman or gentlewoman possesses. What is a light belief? Well suppose I am sitting at the breakfast table. Before me, in the newspaper is a picture of the Loch Ness monster. I may look at it and say to myself "Goodness! That might just be a monster after all!" I then continue with my breakfast. This is a lightly ironic mood in which I maintain, for a brief instant, the conviction that the world may be a far stranger place than is commonly assumed. This mood is one which I consider a small but essential aspect of an educated outlook on the world. One might call it skepticism or, if one prefers, skepticism about skepticism.[38] Of course, on one influential account of belief, the pragmatist one, a belief should issue in a habit or disposition of some kind: still, as even Pierce admits, a habit need not be deep but only persistent such as the habit of giving the bus driver 5 pennies instead of a nickel. (Pierce, 119) I will say then in good pragmatist fashion that stories of the strange and monstrous cause me to perk up my ears hopefully but little else.

One might maintain such a mood about any number of things such as

---

[38]The master of this mood is American writer Charles Fort who spent his life obsessively collecting tales of the anomalous and apparently inexplicable. One wonders though if a light belief is truly honored by making it such serious business. Sasquatch and Nessie rightly shun the earnest searchers who seek to photograph them. Their 'discovery' after all would simply render them 'animals' in the usual sense and objects of ordinary study. The crypto-biologist would have to give over his subject to 'normal science' as practiced by standard biology! A delightful account of Fort and a host of other eccentrics may be found in Martin Gardner's Fads and Fallacies in the Name of Science. Perhaps even more entertaining (because less moralistic) is Can You Speak Venusian? By Sir Patrick Moore.

ghosts, ESP, Tarot cards or palm reading. However, it occurs to me that I might be willing to commit myself to more than the claim that a superstition or two is something the worldly wise may keep in their back pockets, if only because of what Hamlet told Horatio. Among our light beliefs there may be some that are more solid than we have been led to think. Epistemic puritans may be outraged at this: after all ghosts and palm reading and the like are prima facie examples of superstition and superstition is a self-evident evil. Yet people continue to believe in them in the face of ridicule and scolding. Pascal says somewhere that the people are wise in their folly. I will argue below that belief in certain seemingly uncanny phenomena can be a form of wise folly. I will do this by considering something from my own back yard: the fairies.

I grew up on Cape Breton Island which is a known habitation of fairies. Oddly, I only discovered this as an adult. There was no fairy lore in my family to speak of. Perhaps we lived too near the highway, I don't know. Whatever the case I was surprised as recently as a few years ago to discover that both the Scots and the indigenous Miq'maw people of Cape Breton agree that its forests are inhabited by mysterious beings who from time to time appear in the form of small humans. To this day one will find, in both communities, people who not only believe in fairies but claim to have encountered them.[39] This latter, apparently, is not a fortunate thing: fairies do not like contact with humans and resent bitterly any prying in their affairs. Moreover they are given to acts of petty vengeance such as tangling the tails of horses, breaking tools, spilling things and generally being a nuisance.[40] At times they will escalate all the way to kidnapping. That said, they are also, I have learned, capable of occasional acts of benevolence. Still, it is considered good policy to give them a wide berth and indeed, to speak of them as little as possible. For this reason they are, like the furies of ancient Greece, not referred to by name but are called the 'little people' or some variant thereof.

Dylan Thomas relates that when asked why he employed fairy rings a Welsh farmer answered "Because I'd be a damn fool if I didn't." (1972; *Collected Poems*, Author's Note) This is an answer worth considering. A wise man hedges his bets against all the forces of contingency fairies included.[41] This is what makes the fascination with fairies of a figure like Arthur Conan

---

[39] For instance Mary Rose and April Julien of Eskasoni Cape Breton who detail their experience in an interview with the CBC program Land and Sea (https://www.youtube.com/watch?v=QLowCTKidZ4). Fairies in Cape Breton seem to be small. In other times and places they are normal sized or even gigantic. It appears that, like Alice, they are indifferent as to extension.

[40] As Shakespeare tells us of Puck: "Are you not he that frights the maidens of the village, skim milk and sometimes labor in the quern and bootless make the breathless housewife churn, and sometimes make the drink to bear no barm, mislead nightwanderers laughing at their harm?" . (MSND, II, I, 35-40)

[41] One might look at it like this, there is the finite circle of our experience and everything outside. The monster, the fairy or what have you stands in for everything outside. This 'outside' is revealed in uncanny events and the word monster itself refers to a revealing or showing as the host is shown in a 'monstrance'. On this general point see W.B. Yeats excellent play The Resurrection.

Doyle ridiculous and censurable. Fairies do not inhabit pleasant Victorian gardens (or gardens of any kind) but are creatures of the wild or near wild. Conan Doyle's fairies displease because they are sentimental garden ornaments. Fairies however are not part of the social ecology of genteel society but of those who live at the edges of nature and wrest their living from beneath its shadow. For such people the natural world is confronted directly in its stark otherness from human concerns and wishes. However they do not confront it as a 'dead' thing, as that mathematical abstraction we in the educated west (by a considerable leap of imagination) have come to call 'matter' or 'res extensa'. Nature has its own quasi-human inwardness. We might say that something of nature withdraws from the human world into itself and this inward spiritual face of nature is what we term the fairies.[42] This aspect of nature manifests itself to the human as disruption and potential chaos: indeed, as a friend once said to me, the fairies are what we have come to term chance. They are a power of contingency that overturns the settled processes of human life and community. For those who try to live a settled life of the edge of the wild they are a serious concern indeed. One would be a damn fool to ignore them. [43]

I don't really know what this has to do with the audio and visual effects that are said to accompany encounters with fairies. I have never dreamt or hallucinated anything with the vividness of fairy stories so I am not terribly moved when such things are proffered as explanations. Visions so odd, it seems to me, should be products of fever, or drug taking or perhaps the effects of extended alcohol abuse. Yet people I have heard speak about the fairies seem to be as much in possession of their faculties as I am.[44] The

---

[42]In the Philosophy of History Hegel tells us: "The position of curious surmise, of attentive eagerness to catch the meaning of nature, is indicated to us in the comprehensive idea of Pan. To the Greeks Pan did not represent the objective Whole, but that indefinite neutral ground which involves the element of the subjective; he embodies that thrill which pervades us in the silence of the forests..." (235)

[43]Fairies appear to be transcultural entities. Indigenous North Americans, Celts and Scandinavians all appear to accept their reality. Indeed, they have status under the law in Iceland. It is not impossible that cultural dissemination explains this peculiar fact but when one adds the fairy like being s of other cultures, such as the nymphs and dryads of the Greeks, it seems plausible to think this is a belief that responds to a deeply felt human need. If one tried to identify this need perhaps it would be the desire to commune with the spirit of the land one inhabits: to relate to it not as an 'it' but as a 'thou', a 'for itself' rather than an 'in itself'. Perhaps too fairy lore concerns the tension in life between the quotidian and the ideal as in Yeats' play Land of the Heart's Desire. At any rate, here are the words of a man who knew a thing or two on the subject: "The magic of Faerie is not an end in itself, its virtue is in its operations: among these are the satisfaction of certain primordial human desires. One of these desires is to survey the depths of space and time. Another is (as will be seen) to hold communion with other living things. A story may thus deal with the satisfaction of these desires, with or without the operation of either machine or magic, and in proportion as it succeeds it will approach the quality and have the flavor of fairy-story." (J.R.R. Tolkien ://www.excellence-in-literature.com/wp-content/uploads/2013/10/fairystoriesbytolkien.pdf) (5)

[44]In this they seem to me distinct from devotees of U.F.O.'s and aliens who ooze paranoia and conspiratorial thinking. Belief in the little people seems on the whole a healthy one. The U.F.O cult on the other hands strikes me (as it did Carl Jung) as reflective of some imbalance in the contemporary psyche. For Jung's account of this see U.F.O's and the Unconscious. At any rate the propensity to hallucinate does not

explanations offered above are not impossible I suppose but I do not tend
to the view that phenomena so widely attested and well defined are pathological in origin (anyway what does it mean to call something pathological
that has been in most times and most places normal?). However, humans
are artists and as a perfectly natural gift or talent some of them may have
a capacity for what could be called 'eidetic visualization'.[45] The English
poet William Blake seems to have had this in spades and was in my humble
opinion all the better for it. Blake could summon images of prophets and
angels of such intensity that they appeared to his own sight. These images
he held to be imaginative realization of transcendent truth: they were no
more 'there' before him than they were simply projections of his mind: they
were 'Giant forms' or spiritual archetypes that opened to us the visions of
eternity. They were as 'trans-objective' as they were 'trans-subjective' being representations of a spiritual realm beyond the ordinary oppositions of
reflective consciousness.

Here we might as well cite Blake further. In the prologue to his poem
Europe the speaker converses as follows with a fairy: "Then tell me, what
is the material world, and is it dead? He laughing answer'd: I will write a
book on leaves of flowers, If you will feed me on love-thoughts, & give me
now and then a cup of sparkling poetic fancies; so when I am tipsie, I'll
sing to you to this soft lute; and shew you all alive the world, when every
particle of dust breathes forth its joy." (*Europe: A Prophecy*, 1978; 13-18)
For Blake, imagination or artistic vision has the power to transform the
world before us from dead mechanism into a ream saturated with life and
purpose.[46] Many passages in his work attest to the power of imagination
to achieve the vision of the world as an organic living whole. This power
may well exist in ordinary people as well as in artistic geniuses: someone
coming upon a mysterious patch of forest one might be wrought to such a
pitch of feeling by its beauty and terror as to visualize externally the object
of their heightened state of consciousness. In a similar way the mystic may
encounter the un-nameable essence of God in scents, lights, music and so
on. This is an imaginative realization of nature in its otherness (yet also
in its mysterious kinship for the form of the fairy is human) that I suspect
is close kin to our poetic faculty. Perhaps it lies at the origin of our poetic

---

seem to bear any necessary relationship to the propensity to hallucinate things that
are culturally significant and well defined parts of an accepted ontology. In other words,
whatever hallucinatory effects exist function as raw material for a complex cultural event.

[45]So Peter Ackroyd speculates in his biography of Blake. (24-25)

[46]Here let me quote some verses of Blake's from a letter to Thomas Butts: "Each
grain of sand, Every stone on the land, Each rock and each hill, Each fountain and rill,
Each herb and each tree, Mountain hill earth and sea, Cloud meteor and star, Are men
seen afar... " (20-30) This deeply animistic vision no doubt has roots in Renaissance
Platonism but the human-form-in- nature Blake hymns here seems to echo the 'fairy-
faith'. One must provide a caveat however: from Blake's radical perspective nature is
radically humanized such that there is no place for any notion of taboo. The fairies
though, in the traditional understanding, involve the notion of the forbidden, that which
is not at the disposal of the human world. For Blake all nature is radically open to
human consciousness, a fact dramatically if disturbingly illustrated by Orc's rape of the
daughter of Urthona in America.

faculty. As Blake tells us in another of his works: "the ancient Poets animated all sensible objects with Gods or Geniuses, calling them by the names and adorning them with the properties of woods, rivers, mountains, lakes, cities, nations, and whatever their enlarged & numerous senses could perceive... " (1978; *On the Marriage of Heaven and Hell*,11,1-10)

Part of my belief in fairies then is my conviction that we have pathologized and stigmatized a perfectly healthy function of the mind. Part of it is my belief that my ancestors of a hundred years ago were responding to the natural world in a way fundamentally true to how they experienced it. What is more, in indigenous communities like the Miq'maw this form of apprehending and relating to nature persists to this day. I say this fully aware that for me the woods contain only plants and animals as we in the west ordinarily define them. If I were to speak in terms of the correspondence theory of truth, I would probably say there are no fairies 'out there'.[47] Perhaps, then, the fairies are among my light beliefs only. Still, I do not begrudge the people of Eskasoni their visions of tiny forest people. In an age when ecological issues loom so large it might even be worth considering radical alternatives to our way picturing nature and our relationship to it. This could well involve a sober second look at (long despised) folkloric traditions and the (even more despised) beliefs of indigenous peoples. If these are folly they are shrewd folly. The fairies, nymphs and river gods of old may be the pressing business of the new millennium: where else might we find a counterweight to the standard conception of nature as a 'standing reserve' of energy waiting simply upon human use?[48] I am no Blake and I don't have forest visions of any kind but one needn't assume this represents some a-historically valid norm as opposed to an accident of time and place: if people see things otherwise, if there are forms of life or ways of relating that include fairies among the things one must deal with, I am happy to listen and maybe, ever so lightly, believe.

---

[47] But of course this is too simple. If instead of using words like contingency, arbitrariness and chance we simply said 'crow' or 'trickster' the fundamental content of our assertions would alter only partly if at all. Fairies are as 'out there' as the phenomena that evoke the use of the word. To cite Quine: "Physical objects are conceptually imported into the situation as convenient intermediaries-not by definition in terms of experience, but simply as irreducible posits comparable, epistemologically, to the gods of Homer." (1205) Quine goes on to tell us he prefers the "myth of physical objects" to the gods of Homer and up to a point I agree. I find however that there are some contexts where the gods of Homer and indeed fairies are as good or better.

[48] Perhaps the reductio ad absurdum of this view is the opinion I once heard a fisherman express that shrimp left in the water due to quota cuts were a form of 'waste'. I do not blame this gentlemen however as our whole western way of relating to nature as potential energy waiting to be converted into work commits us to this very proposition. On this point see Heidegger's The Question Concerning Technology: "The revealing thatrules throughout modern technology has the character of a setting -upon, in the sense of a challenging -forth. Such challenging happens in that the energy concealed in nature is unlocked, what is unlocked is transformed, what is transformed is stored up, what is stored up is in turn distributed, and what is distributed is switched about ever anew." (http://www2.hawaii.edu. TheQuestionConcerningTechnology.pdf") (5)

5 GOD

The purpose of this essay is not to prove the existence of God though a proof
is what it contains. Rather, I will try to argue that Atheism and Theism
stand or fall together. By this I mean that a common history sustains
them both: at the basis of this history lies something I am tempted to
call Latinity. It is something the philosopher Martin Heidegger also called
'onto-theology'. This term (and what exactly Heidegger meant by it) is of
course controversial so I will only give it the broadest interpretation here.
By onto-theology I refer to a core assumption of Western (Latin) theology
according to which being and thinking are identical in god. In Augustine,
Aquinas, Scotus and others we find the argument that god is first and
foremost the act of being, 'to be' rather than a being. Eastern (Greek)
theology does not make this assumption finding 'being' to be a secondary
determination of the divine as it proceeds from itself into creation. To speak
somewhat roughly, this is the distinction between Aristotle's doctrine that
god is *nous noeseos* (self- thinking thought) and Plato's doctrine that God
or the Good is *huperousias* or beyond being and knowledge. Obviously
those who follow the first path will have a more rationalist bent than those
who follow the second. The Western doctrine elevates being to identity
with thinking so that, as Parmenides said, it is the same thing to think as
to be.[49] This entails that thought and being mutually condition each other
and that principles of thought are at the same time conditions of being
(Descartes' invocation of the *cogito* might be taken as a watershed in this
tradition). Thus, what cannot be thought cannot be and what-cannot-not-
be thought must be. Thus, God either exists because he must or does not
exist because he cannot. God is either necessary or impossible (I take it
as established that a conditional entity would not be what we mean by the
word God though some may differ).

It might be interesting then to consider whether the existence of god
is impossible. Dogmatic atheism as opposed to mere agnosticism would
have it so. Of course some atheists such as Dawkins would have it that the

---

[49] "Thinking and the thought that it is are the same. For not without what is, in
which it is expressed, will you find thinking." (34-35) Malebranche is most direct on the
subject: "The idea of being without restriction, of the infinite, of generality, is not the
idea of creatures, or the essence that pertains to them: it is the idea which represents
the Deity, or the essence that pertains to it. All particular beings participate in being,
but no particular being is identical with it." (162)

existence of God is only astronomically unlikely. This does not seem to me to change the terms of the argument. Laws of thought condition what is probable or improbable as much as they condition what is or is not. If one takes the typically Latin Western tradition that thought determines being by determining what is possible to be one will inevitably form the view that reason informs the question of God either positively or negatively, one will trade in proof or disproof of Divine existence. Thus in western thought we find what we do not always find in eastern thought: the notion that the existence/nonexistence of God is a determination of discursive rationality rather than mystical experience, say, or some other mode of knowledge. God is a postulate of reason either theoretical or (as in Kant) practical. The relevance of this history to the history of western atheism at least in its positivistic form seems clear as Secular Humanists, for instance, insist with almost puritanical zeal that our beliefs must be grounded on reason especially as it is embodied in the methods of the sciences. We might call this 'classical' Atheism to distinguish it from post-modern or existentialist forms of Atheism (which, as the case of Derrida shows, are not easy to disentangle from the so-called 'negative theology!). It is the form of Atheism dictated by the history of Western rationalism and its epigones in the various 'philosophies of language' that dominated the 20th century. It is also the form of Atheism most prominent in the Anglo-Saxon world.

What can be said for Classical Atheism? The case for it was put with perfect exactitude by Thomas Aquinas. In his *Summa of Theology* he gives two fundamental considerations that tell decisively against the existence of God (which later in the same article he will defend by means of the famous 'five ways'). The first one concerns the problem of evil. Aquinas tells us that any attribute expressed to infinity annihilates its contrary. Thus, heat in an absolute degree would annihilate the very possibility of cold: contraries limit each other so that taken to infinity they must exclude each other. (1997; Q.2, A.3) This means that God, being infinite goodness, must annihilate his contrary evil. However we observe evil in the world. Therefore, God cannot exist. There is fair bit of *a priori* structure to unpack here but let me keep it simple. What Aquinas is pointing to here is the logical structure of what we call contrariety. Indeed the argument he gives has the characteristic structure we have labeled disjunctive syllogism: A or B, but A therefore not-B. Philosophers do not wonder about such things as much as they should. My students though sometimes find it odd that something called the disjunctive syllogism should sit in judgment on reality. Where is it enthroned? From whence does it issue its implacable decrees on what is and is not without, it would seem, existing itself? Well, for Aquinas these laws of thought are given within being itself: being dictates to thought its laws the first of which is the law of non-contradiction or the law that what is, is and is not at the same time what is not. This is the principle that lies at the root of the disjunctive syllogism.[50] Again we seem

---

[50]Of course Christian theologians have, particularly in their speculations on the Trinity, developed a relational logic of personhood that cuts across the conventional determinations of metaphysics. This is a logic of co-inherence rather than a logic of binary

to be Parmenideans: to be and to be thought is one and the same.

Rock-ribbed Thomists may not be pleased with me but I am tempted here to formulate a retorsive argument. In the ordinary empirical world a thought seems one thing and a thing another. We *apply* rules of logic, mathematical concepts, canons of thinking etc. *to* the empirical without asking where the connection between them lies. What is a law of thought that apples and oranges, elephants and kittens must obey it? The process of thinking seems to presume some connection between the two: positing causes without necessity seems to violate the principle that nature contains no superfluity for instance. Indeed, this is Aquinas' second objection to the existence of God. Nature, he opines, is a self-sustaining chain of natural causes in which every finite event finds its adequate ground in some other finite event. Nature is self-explanatory and the existence of God a superfluous hypothesis. (Q. 3, A2) This of course is the view that Aquinas refutes in his famous (yet ill-understood) five ways. Crude caricatures of the five ways have been refuted (and defended!) over and over for centuries yet Aquinas' core ontological insight, that everything in nature is an unresolved duality of act/potency, essence/existence, necessity/contingency and so on that depend upon a prior unity in God seems to me compelling. In a way it is the central ontological insight of the Platonic tradition itself: that the dualism of form and instance is resolved in the unity of the Good. I add the proviso however that Aquinas' consideration of the existence of God unfolds under the sign of being and that this distinguishes his from other Platonisms both ancient and modern.[51]

However I am going to take a different tack here as it is not my aim to delve so deeply in the history of ontology and try the patience of readers who do not characteristically think in such terms. Rather than a historical disquisition I will briefly discuss a logical point. As we have seen thinking things under the sign of being imposes certain limitations. We have seen that the disjunctive syllogism is one. Another is causality: the fact that being cannot come from non-being entails that beings are grounded in other beings. Disjunction again poses a fundamental limit. The logical expression of this limit is the principle of sufficient reason: beings must be grounded

---

difference that expresses the underlying unity of superficially opposed determinations. Of course the notion that opposition is predicated on an underlying identity is as old as Heraclitus though it is perhaps Hegel who develops this notion with the greatest thoroughness and finesse in modern times. We might say of the principle of contradiction, then, that it is a principle of finite discourse. Even for the Medieval Scholastics God known as the first principle of Being (object of the science of metaphysics) is not God as known to himself nor as revealed to humanity in sacred history but a dim participation thereof.

[51] As Aquinas puts it: "Now since God is very being by his own essence, created being must be his own proper effect; as to ignite is the proper effect of fire. Now god causes this effect in things not only when they first begin to be, but as long as they are preserved in being; as light is caused in the air by the sun as long as the air remains illuminated. Therefore, as long as a thing has being, God must be present to it, according to its mode of being. But Being is innermost in each thing and most fundamentally inherent in all things since it is formal (actual) in respect of everything found in a thing... Hence it must be that God is in all things, and innermostly. (I,8,1) The reader can meditate with profit on the beautiful metaphors Aquinas uses in this passage.

in that which is sufficient to produce them i.e. other beings. Conversely, we have the principle of parsimony: being is sufficient ground for beings: once the being of one thing is accounted for by the being of another one need appeal to no other principle. Sufficient reason must be found yet at the same time reason is sufficient to account for what is. Thus we have the ground for atheism. Evil cannot arise from nothing; if it exists it arises from some cause. If god exists god is that cause, yet this is impossible because opposite excludes opposite. Moreover the being of nature (the sum total of things) is adequate to account for what is in nature, therefore there is no reason to appeal any cause prior to it. We have a tidy little circle, being is both necessary to account for being and adequate to account for being, we neither fall short of nor exceed it.

As a result of this Atheism is as ontological a position as Theism: it appeals to being to deny the divine being. Is Atheism also the same as theism? Does it rest on the assumption that the being of beings is divine being? I think it does. Here we must think carefully. Nietzsche says to get rid of God we must get rid of grammar.[52] We must get rid of the notion of a logos or intelligible structure that determines thinking and being. To allow this would be to allow a unity of thinking and being and bring back the Platonic good or the ontological God of Aquinas or Descartes (it might even be to bring back, horror of horrors, the moral God of Kant!). This is because there is no unity between the determinations of thought and being from the finite side: Hume showed this inescapably in his critique of induction. We can never demonstrate that finite categories of thought determine reality from within those categories as generations of skeptics have shown. The unity of thinking and being must be given absolutely in the divine if it is to be given at all. Yet Atheism in its rationalistic form presumes this very unity as we have showed above, the argument of the atheist presumes the logos given in being. In Nietzsche's terms it presumes grammar. In Christian terms it presumes the first and second persons of the Trinity. The existence of god appears to be a transcendental condition of the possibility of Atheism.

Thus both theism and atheism presuppose the western history of being and both are grounded (one in a self-contradictory fashion) in the unity of thinking and being in God. If you like Atheism and Theism stand or fall with the western account of being. Of course many would argue that this fall would be a welcome thing. They would argue that we need new accounts of God that are not trapped in the ontological circle and a freer encounter with the divine that is not bound up in 'rationalistic' thinking. Some look to the older forms of Platonism for this new account and others to the existentialist

---

[52] "'Reason' in language- oh what an old deceptive female she is! I am afraid we are not rid of God because we still have faith in grammar" . (Twilight of the Idols, 483) The context of this quote is a discussion of what Nietzsche takes to be a cardinal error of the Greeks: the positing of a rational intelligible structure behind the apparent chaos of appearances that stands to appearance as its truth and ground. In this sense of course the rationalistic atheism of a Dawkins or Dennett scarcely constitutes a rejection of theism. The latter in fact believes in a 'substrate neutral algorithm' that determines the structure of all natural (including cultural) events. A 'logos' if ever there was one.

and phenomenological traditions. Presumably this new spirituality would allow for new forms of Atheism as well: forms not so dependent on western 'reason' and thus open to the objections I have here put forward. Many are busy articulating just these sorts of positions. I cannot weigh in here on their efforts: probably I am too old school to do it well! My brief paper has only served to show that there is an old Atheism which is certainly as dead as the old God seems to be. So called 'New Atheism' is precisely this old Atheism in a louder voice. Its shrillness no doubt comes from its complete irrelevance to the serious thinking occurring in our epoch. It is a timid retreat into the old certainties of the Western ontology, both its scientific rationalism and its imperialist politics. The latter have come at last to total grief in the current debacle in the Middle East. The former cannot even keep creationism out of high school textbooks.[53] Atheism may find it as refreshing as theism to think outside the ontological box.

---

[53] Secular humanists can of course win every single argument concerning Darwinism. What they cannot do is make people in Georgia or Alabama care. Part of me suspects that the reason for this is that the form of reason they espouse is inescapably a bourgeois phenomenon: the reason of a technocratic managerial class. Various rural, urban and regional underclasses (who have a shrinking stake in the bourgeois economic order) have less and less to lose by rejecting its standards of public rationality for the wilder reaches of myth and imagination. The latter may be seen on full display in the Creation Museum in Petersburg Kentucky. A corresponding phenomenon would be the fondness for conspiracy theories among rappers and other spokesmen for the urban black underclass.

6 Why Religious Faith and Scientific Faith are (Roughly!) the Same

It is a sad fact about the human condition that we need to know far more than we can actually understand. I have never personally drunk a cup of bleach. Nor do I understand much of the chemical composition of bleach or the reactions it forms with human flesh. I have been told though that it is a bad idea. Having no idea really what I'm talking about I tell my children exactly what was told to me. This gives me pause. There is one thing I do know more than a bit about and that is the dialogues of Plato. Many of the things people who haven't read the dialogues of Plato think about their author and his views (if they think of him at all) strike me as either misconceptions or oversimplifications. This gives me pause for I am in the exact same position as the non-reader of Plato with respect to vast tracts of human knowledge. Knowing how wrong people can be about my little area of specialty does not give me much confidence about my own assumptions with respect to astronomy, chemistry, ornithology and so on. Still, I have opinions on these subjects of a half-baked sort. Writing in the *Atlantic Monthly* (2015; Nov.24), Paul Bloom labels these sorts of beliefs credences. Credences are not very accurate, generally, but the sorry truth is we cannot do without them this side of heaven. The range of our opinions outstrips our actual knowledge because life makes demands that are complex and multi-faceted.

Recognizing that this is so Mr. Bloom still wants to defend the proposition that the sciences should have some special authority for us even though as individuals we may be ignorant of almost all of what they contain. For Bloom the sciences are worthy objects of credence even when we lack the expertise to evaluate what specialists in various fields are saying. Bloom contrasts this with the credences given to religious doctrines which he holds to be in a fundamentally different category. Religious faith he tell us is not scientific faith. What he seems to mean by this is that faith in the sciences is earned faith while, presumably, religious faith is unearned faith. Science has earned our credence, he tells us, for the following reasons: "... scientific practices – observation and experiment; the development of falsifiable hypotheses; the relentless questioning of established views- have proven uniquely powerful in revealing the surprising underlying structure of the world we live in... " By way of contrast he notes that "Religion has no equivalent record of discovering hidden truths." For this reason he affirms that science is not just "... one faith community among many. It has earned its epistemological stripes. And when the stakes are high, as they are with climate change and vaccines, we should appreciate its special status."

Apart from his reference to Karl Popper's now hopelessly discredited 'falsifiability principle' I don't begrudge Mr. Bloom his enthusiasm for science.[54] In many ways it HAS earned our credence. However the implication that it has uniquely earned our credence strikes me as manifestly false. I'm sure Mr. Bloom would agree that students of literature add much to our knowledge of authors by testing their ideas about them against their texts. Indeed I'm sure we should trust the impressions of people who have spent their lives reading Joyce over the impressions we form from reading one story from *Dubliners*. However, I suspect Mr. Bloom is not terribly interested in whether classicists or Joyce scholars have earned our credence. His real point surely is that religions have *not* earned our credence because they have no record of discovery about the world. If this is the case Mr. Bloom is living a curiously sheltered life in his psychology department because religions have in fact discovered plenty not about the physical world but about the human condition.[55] Here are some things 'discovered' by the religion of ancient Greece: that justice is different from revenge, that justice is giving others their due and that humans beings must suffer before they learn. Here are some things discovered by Buddhism: that existence is suffering, that life is impermanence and that enlightenment brings compassion. Here are things discovered by the ancient Hebrew religion: that the word has an intelligible structure as God's creation, that justice is for strangers as well as friends, that the weak are objects of concern as much as the strong. To this we may add Jesus' discovery that personhood is the object of unconditional moral concern and Islam's discovery that we make idols of the things around us every bit as false as stone and wooden gods (the sin of shirk). Thanks to the religious ferment that occurred in the Ancient World beginning around the 8th Century B.C.E. they are now part of the human patrimony: they constitute a body of wisdom that is known as much through practice as it is apprehended intellectually.

---

[54] Scientists though, like theologians, sometimes offer contradictory positions, as all of us avid coffee drinkers are keenly aware. In this case do we trust in science to ultimately resolve the dispute? If we do which scientist do we trust in the meantime? There are some problems with treating 'Science' as a substantive. I suppose though we could repose our trust not in 'science' exactly but in scientific consensus though that may be overturned on a semi-regular basis.

[55] I must note that religious people (if not religions) have a considerable record of discovery and invention even in the technical sphere. Almost all the basic solutions for human living (toolmaking, hunting, agriculture, fire, writing, building and so on) were found when people were animists and lived in a world saturated with spirits. Religion, at least, did not dull their wits and for all this author knows may well have contributed to these discoveries.

What I am saying of course is that however deficient they may be individually collectively the religions of the world have 'discovered' much of the moral and spiritual wisdom of humankind.[56] This has nothing to do with accepting or rejecting these faiths in a confessional sense: nor does it even have to do with believing all the propositions set out above. I am not a Buddhist in any sense yet I have learned a great deal about myself from Buddhism. Some of this is through finding in Buddhism things with which I agree. Just as important however are the things I have learned from disagreeing with profoundly thought out and deeply felt positions not my own. Thus, in Mr. Bloom's sense the world's religions (at their best) have earned my credence: when I pick up the *Upanishads*, or the *Gospels* or *Antigone* I am quite confident that I will discover something new about myself and the human condition as a whole. What I am not likely to discover is much information about the natural world though I may here and there discover some (it was from Homer that I learned that cows have beautiful eyes, much to my shame as I grew up around cows!). The unstated premise of Mr. Bloom's argument seems to be that the physical world is the proper object of knowledge and only those disciplines that tell us about it produce knowledge. This is a view of knowledge that is falsified daily (if Mr. Bloom wants to speak about falsification) in every Arts department in the land.

There are essential truths about our-selves that are the province of literature, philosophy and, maligned though it is, religion. This is because along with quantifiable knowledge of the object world there is introspective knowledge of the human condition. I would suggest then that scientific faith and religious faith are indeed roughly comparable. I have developed a sort of trust in the sacred books and great poems of the world as I have in the great works of philosophy: those who give themselves to them will get back as much or more than they put in. This trust is not indefeasible of course but neither is trust in the scientific experts in which Mr. Bloom and indeed all of us perforce put our trust. He says, as I do, that over time and in spite of the inevitable failures it is better to repose trust in certain things than not. Thus, I hold that my faith in the sacred traditions of human kind is no different at the end of the day than Mr. Bloom's trust of the sciences. Nothing is more preposterous than the impression created by people like Richard Dawkins or P.Z. Myers that books like the Bible are gibberish strung randomly together: a proposition as absurd and ignorant as anything put forward by the most deluded creationist. Anyone who knows how to read myths and sagas (and yes that is a skill that needs to be learned) can easily and quickly see this to be true. Indeed they will quickly

---

[56]By 'discovery' I here mean 'embodied in exemplary form'. I do not mean to imply the banal claim that Jesus, say, had only novel ideas or that Siddartha Gautama was without spiritual precedent of any kind. Truth is like the proverbial barn door. Few nail the center of it but most hit it somewhere. Yet truths that are vague or implicit or scattered among many sources can attain a peculiar intensity of expression in canonical texts and/or exemplary lives and this is the form in which we tend to encounter them. For instance, self-knowledge is a broadly treated theme but if someone told me they possessed it perfectly it would be to Oedipus Rex that I would point them to correct their error.

see that the most fundamental questions human beings can ask themselves are first posed in mythic form. At very least then Mr. Bloom owes us some explanation as to why he thinks we come away from the *Oresteia* or the *Bhagavad Gita* precisely as ignorant about the world as when we picked them up. Can the claim that no crucial 'discoveries' or 'disclosures' can be credited to religion really survive any but the most jaundiced and inept reading of the world's sacred texts? To be frank, is there anything essential about the human condition that cannot be discovered, say, in the first four chapters of *Genesis*?

It occurs to me however that the comments above may not persuade the more committed secular humanist. Perhaps you think I am committing a certain kind of fraud. People who are naïve about modern art or avant-garde music often think that those who claim to admire it are pretentious fakes who only *pretend* to like works by Kandinsky or Stockhausen which, any sensible person can immediately discern, are random splashes of color or meaningless noise. Likewise certain Humanists seem to believe that texts like the book of *Genesis* contain a string of discredited *facts* that 'theologians' only pretend to find other meanings in. Sam Harris seems to be one of these people: in his book *The End of Faith* he claims that he can find the same 'esoteric meanings' in a recipe book that Sufis, say, find in the Koran. (2005; 287) The only argument I can think of to answer this concern is a practical test. I propose in the second section of this essay to show the reader how *I* read a religious text (from the Hebrew Bible) so that the reader can judge for herself whether the meanings I elicit have emerged naturally from that text or whether I have spun my interpretation out of thin air. The result, I hope, will be to show that responsible reading differs from painful literalism *and* from interpretive anarchy.[57]

Before I do this however there is a crucial point I must make about the *modern* study of the bible. The modern reader of the Bible, if they are a critical reader, takes careful note of the genre of different texts. For instance the Bible contains Mythology, Saga, Legend, Prophecy, Lyric poetry, Chronicle and so on. Some of these genres, like chronicle or history do bear some rough relation to factual content. Others obviously do not, such as myth and lyric poetry. Also, the Bible, like any text, contains a high level of figurative language such as simile and metaphor. Thus, as Augustine

---

[57]This is Harris at his absolute silliest. The ancient traditions of spiritual and esoteric reading of sacred texts in the Christian, Jewish and Islamic worlds are not in fact the exercises in wild eisegesis they are often portrayed as, a fact more and more scholars are coming to recognize. If any reader wants to consult serious scholarship on this question I would recommend they begin by perusing Henri de Lubac's magisterial study Medieval Exegesis (now available in English translation). There are many comparable works on Islamic and Jewish hermeneutical traditions. Harris seems to have inspired a host of online atheists with his literalism. Consider the typical anti-theistic denizen of the web. He has read, he claims, the Bible and the Quran many times and regards his immediate, untutored reactions to these texts as direct manifestations of his superior insight. For this reason, he requires no secondary study to grasp anything, particularly anything textual. This is because texts simply say what they mean. Keats' Ode on a Grecian Urn is a description of a pot. He is the first to discover the simple, sublime truth that interpretation is a sham and that a talking snake is never anything but a talking snake.

says, any student of the Bible must understand the nature and function of various figures of speech.[58] However we must also take note of the genre of the work we are considering. Thus, we may ask whether worrying about the physical location of Noah's ark, say, or whether it could accommodate dinosaurs is really appropriate to the kind of story we are studying. Since this story obviously has the characteristics of what below I will call an etiological myth I think the answer is clearly no. Fundamentalists alas consider all stories in the Bible to be historical documents but with all due respect I cannot see how this could be true or, for that matter, interesting if it was. More surprising to me is the fact that so many Atheists seem to agree with them and naively criticize the biblical texts as historic or scientific documents as if that were the only form of significance they could have.

I will begin with a familiar bit of text: the story of Noah from the *Book of Genesis*. The story is one familiar from many cultures. It is clearly modelled on the tale of Utnapishtim from the Sumerian *Epic of Gilgamesh*. A very similar story is also told by Ovid in his *Metamorphoses* although this source is later than the Hebrew Bible. Now at this point the more red-blooded humanist will thunder that the Hebrew text is obviously plagiarized from the Sumerian original and is thus a pious fraud. I ask him to be patient however: those of us who read literature often encounter something we call intertextuality. This refers to the fact that stories and poems and novels often contain references to other stories and poems and novels. These references are often a form of subtle commentary and can contain important clues to the meaning of a text. For example Sterne's *Tristram Shandy* contains a number of references to *Don Quixote* by Cervantes: clearly, Sterne would like us to consider these two texts together when we interpret his novel. Similarly, I will show that the Hebrew text actually wants us to consider the Sumerian original of which it is not a mindless copy but a *creative retelling* that alters the original in a number of interesting ways. Thus, texts like *Genesis* and *Gilgamesh* can be read as if engaged in conversation with each other.

The best way to begin is to consider the Sumerian story first. The story concerns a man named Utnapishtim who, alone among mortals, has cheated death. The basic parameters of the Noah story are laid out here. We have the notion of a global inundation caused by the wrath of the gods. We have the notion of a just man and his family who are, as it were, an epitome of humankind saved from the general wreckage. (1972;108) We even have an epitome of the natural world saved within an ark. (108) The story of Utnapishtim is thus very familiar to us. In some ways however it is less so. Being saved from the deluge Utnapishtim does not return to the

---

[58] Indeed Augustine says that the entire panoply of secular knowledge is implied in the effort to read the sacred text for even to construe the basic sense we need an understanding of grammar, rhetoric, mathematics, logic, basic science and so on. This kind of basic interpretive work has the virtue of narrowing the range of possible readings of the text to a number manageable by the critic as we can, say, exclude all readings that violate grammar, that misconstrue figures like metonymy or hyperbole and so on. Augustine lays out the fundamentals of Scriptural hermeneutics in the concluding three books of On Christian Doctrine.

ordinary struggle of existence. Rather he is granted immortality in a kind of never-land where death does not intervene but where life and growth seem absent. (107) Moreover the motivation for the flood seems very different. The Sumerian gods act out of malaise; bored and tired with the noise and chaos of creation they yearn for silence and repose (whereas the younger gods and humans enjoy their bustling activity). (108) Nor have we any assurance at the end of the tale that global catastrophe will not recur. All in all it is a very pessimistic tale. The universe seems only contingently on the side of human flourishing and development. Indeed, a 'death wish' seems to underlie cosmic order itself. This is in fact a very sophisticated guess about the nature of things with parallels in contemporary physics. It is not however a consoling one: it offers us an alternative of universal death and decay as a permanent possibility (perhaps a certainty) or a parody of eternal life in the form of an endless (and endlessly tedious) temporal existence. Clearly, this story is intended to confront us with the tragic dimension of existence and carefully undermines any consolation we may seek by making both death and physical immortality equally unendurable.

It may be that the ancient Sumerians saw a noble resolution in facing the darkest truths of life. From the text we have I find it hard to say. However if we turn to the Hebrew story we find some startling differences. The first thing I note is that the story has a very unusual, perhaps even paradoxical structure. Its form is that of an etiological myth: it tells the story of how something came to be the case. In this case it seeks the origin of a covenant between humanity and God according to which the universe will not end by catastrophe. (*Genesis*, 1990; 9,12-16) It also explains the origin of certain universal ethical intuitions we have about the sanctity of life (what we would now call 'natural law'). (9, 4-6) However, the means by which it does so seems odd. It reassures us against the possibility of a universal deluge by telling the story of a universal deluge. This reminds us of another etiological myth, the story of Abraham and Isaac, which tells the story of why the Jews do not practice human sacrifice. It does this by telling the story of an attempted human sacrifice. This may have no significance beyond being a characteristic trope of Hebrew story telling: a neat trick for structuring a good tale. Perhaps it has some deeper significance, we shall see. For now let us note a few things. Firstly, the divine motivation is figured differently. Specifically, it is a response to the scale of the violence and bloodshed that, sadly, we have come to know is deeply, perhaps inexpugnably, part of the human condition. (6, 11-12) We might, to explore the metaphor that seems to me to be lurking here, take the scale and ferocity of a universal deluge as the only means adequate to wash the stain of blood from the earth. When the ancient commentators associated the waters of the flood with the cleansing and purging waters of baptism perhaps they were not far off the mark. If we add the observation that life and renewal presuppose a sort of death we would get even closer to the ancient understanding of this text: indeed we may take this text as revealing that aspect of the divine that embodies itself in acts of creative destruction (rather like the Hindu Shiva).

In spite of the external violence of the tale (as in fairy tales the narrative makes no assumption that the universe conforms to the moral intuitions of 21st Century readers) the conclusion of the Hebrew tale is fairly optimistic. Noah is not, like Utnapishtim, shuffled off to a tedious immortality. He is rather returned to history. Moreover, and here we have the core of the story, he receives from God an intensification of the law that has hitherto guided humankind. Respect for the sanctity of human life is now a specific object of legislation. This legislation is in force not just for God's chosen people but for all human kind. The catastrophic judgment ends in a deepening of the divine human relation and a reaffirmation of the place of the human in creation. We can see then that the Hebrew story intends something very different from its Sumerian counterpart. It means to communicate something that really has little to with whether the dinosaurs had to be juveniles to fit on the ark. This something we can even attach a label to: it could be called proto-humanism by those who like it and anthropocentrism by those who don't. This is the view that humans are something more than a meaningless appendage of nature that the gods can destroy at will. Far from this, in fact, they are central to the created order. Thus, the point of the story is a kind of ironic reversal: through telling an old Sumerian tale about the frightening power and indifference of the Gods the point is made that God and humanity have a special unbreakable bond and covenant: a bond that renders the violent destruction of human life an ultimate evil.

Vis a vis the Sumerian text we may say that the Hebrew story discloses or discovers something new and indeed vital to the progress of human history. By this disclosure (or to use the old word 'revelation') I do not, as I indicated above, necessarily mean something true. You may with some justification think it was the Sumerians who were right all along. For my present purposes it is enough to say that what is disclosed or revealed is a fundamental and permanent *possibility*. It is an epochal event when some great text or work of art or deed injects a new voice in the ongoing conversation that is human culture. It is an epochal event when we are called to attend to *something new*. The Bible, fact, contains many such revelatory moments (such as giving of the Torah to Moses or the founding of the Hebrew monarchy) each instantiating fundamental narrative patterns whose structure constitutes the *deep intentionality* or *deep grammar* of the text: the 'word' that is the ultimate object of interpretation.

In neither case did I approach either *Gilgamesh* or the Hebrew Bible knowing immediately what they meant. After all there is no need to grapple with a text one already understands. In both cases I went through a process of discovery in which I did not, at first, know if I would discover anything. Not that I had any doubt that I would. I was scheduled to lecture on these texts and had no choice! I could not walk into the class the next day and inform the students that my lecture on *Gilgamesh* was cancelled because I could make no sense of it. In almost two decades of teaching this has never happened. I read every text I teach on the assumption I will find something to say about it and I have not yet (knock on wood!) seen this assumption defeated. I refer here to what might be called 'hermeneutic faith'. Hermeneutic faith is something I would compare very closely to scientific faith.

Both perhaps are related to the experience that Aristotle called wonder. One's first reaction to reading *Job*, say, might be a sense of confusion. If it is mere confusion then no doubt one will, as many a frazzled student does, never crack *Job* open again. However there is confusion and rich confusion. Caught up in the poetry and drama of *Job* I may struggle to translate into conscious reflection just what it is that so impresses me. I may feel that my understanding has before it not a paucity of information to process but an excess. The text then becomes for me an object of wonder. I may rest at this stage of course. My takeaway from *Job* would then be a hushed mood of reflection that went no further than aesthetic reverie. It would then correspond to the aesthetic form we call music. However, a wonderful thing happens when one has to teach something. Faced with a roomful of students one has no option but to begin to state discursively (in however inadequate a way) what *Job* is all about. Job becomes an object of analysis and criticism rather than of simple reverence. Hopefully, at the end of this process of analysis the student and teacher together have achieved insight not only into *Job* but into themselves and the world about them. Ideally they will be able to articulate these insights in a reflective form even though there may remain so much more to be said about the text.

This process is sufficiently successful for me that I can, with considerable confidence, take a book of the Hebrew Bible with which I am not very familiar, the *Book of Judges* say, and assign it to my class. I have a teacher's faith in the texts of the ancient Hebrews as I have a teacher's faith in the texts of the ancient Greeks and Romans. This is not indefeasible: the *Book of Habakkuk* may turn out to be one of Judaism's rare duds. Statius may turn out to be not so exciting a poet as one hoped. Still, all things considered, I trust that texts and traditions that have given in the past will continue to give and this seems to me pretty close to a scientist's belief (which can never be a certainty) that having given up its secrets in the past nature will continue to do so. One could perhaps say that I trust in the process of closely reading core texts: it has delivered in the past and I trust (without knowing) that it will deliver in the future. I trust this stance in part because I am always in the midst of it: it is like a fish's belief in water.

A scientist too has faith but it is important to be exact about the nature of this faith. A scientist trusts not so much in a particular fact or theory as in a process for uncovering facts and developing theories.[59] As I trust in

---

[59]People assert again and again that Science differs from religion in demanding evidence for the claims it makes. This however is not true. Scientists certainly do believe in theories on the basis of evidence but scientific theories are in point of fact always underdetermined by this evidence. Even our measurements of 'constants' like the speed of light may be more exact than the thing being measured. Moreover, scientists have many implicit beliefs (like the non-existence of Cartesian demons) which are not even thematic for them let alone justified by evidence. Conversely, people with religious faith constantly offer evidence for the things they believe such as the reliability of ancient documents or the improbability of certain tales being fabrications. This kind of evidence is no better and no worse (in kind at least) than the evidence offered by scientists. Religious beliefs, however, are similarly underdetermined by the putative evidence offered

the process of close reading of texts so does the scientist trust in the process of closely reading nature. Particularly he trusts in the values and methods of scientists to produce satisfying results. Like mine, his faith is grounded in experience both individual and collective. Wonder at nature (a mood cherished by many a poet) has issued in detailed readings of nature. Like the process of close reading described above science has produced these readings consistently over time, in other words it has formed a tradition. These readings have been interesting and successful enough to secure the sciences an exalted place in our society, indeed, a far more exalted place than the study of written texts. Of course, as Hume would point out, none of this precludes the possibility of science starting a long string of failures tomorrow. These failures might be severe enough to put the entire endeavor into question. Similarly, my understanding of the *Odyssey* may crumble next time I teach it. Humans are always on a tightrope where the next moment may witness a fatal plunge: that is simply our condition which a Hebrew author long ago named vanity. We always face the specter of ultimate absurdity even as we carry on in hope. The object of hope in the case of both textual criticism and natural science is the same: the terminal point of dialogue where the differences shade into a unified perception of the text or phenomenon in question. This unified perception may exist only as regulative ideal but it is nonetheless the presupposition of any dialogue that different opinions and outlooks will mutually enrich each other and issue in a richer and truer synthesis of knowledge. We may have no idea, ultimately, if this point exists or is attainable if it does exist but it seems to me the rational faith (to use a Kantian term) of anyone who participates in the inquiry into truth in a communal or dialogical sense. Thus, the scientist, like the reader, trusts that the methodical application of critical thinking will be a slow conquest over the lingering specter of absurdity.

It remains however to consider religious faith more closely. I have spoken about a very broad kind of hermeneutic faith embodied in my own reading practices. Scientific faith is like this except that in one crucial sense it is narrower. Anyone who has a commitment to science in the western world has a commitment not to ancient Greek science or to Chinese science but to Western science. Faith in the intelligibility of the world may also translate into faith into one particular account of that intelligibility: an account that we have hitherto found satisfactory in the things we have asked of it. Realistically though, I doubt very much if the process of induction (which troubled Hume so much) is much at play here (except perhaps as part of the *public rhetoric* of science). Western Science, rather, is something in which the scientist has a developed habit of trust. It is a dispensation the scientist *inhabits*: for instance he or she frames all questions in terms of its reigning theories. By doing so the Scientist also predetermines the range of possible answers. There is nothing particularly surprising or disturbing about this. It is no different than what a Chinese or Indian scientist would

for them: eventually one has to decide to believe in them or not and this is in both science and religion an act of will or if you like a 'leap of faith'.

do. Yet we have also to take into account the fact that Western Science has become a kind of global fact and as such is the norm against which the deviations are measured. It is, if you like, a *social objectivity* for those whose understanding of science conforms to the Baconian equation of knowledge with power.[60] Perhaps what is objective is not so much this or that theory but rather the notion of science as wedded not to pure contemplation but to the conquest of nature by a technocratic society. Western science, like Greek science, is grounded in a certain life stance, one that favors action over contemplation for instance. We might say then that western science has become a more or less universal *project*: a project that is historically and socially situated and has taken (in the West and elsewhere) institutional form.

I think this is quite close to the state of mind in which we prefer a particular religious position to another. Our Western scientist may for instance also be a Christian either in the broad cultural sense that many in the western world are or in the sense of belonging to one of the historical Christian confessions. Let us say that our scientist, John Doe, belongs to the Church of England. The first thing this means is that John Doe is committed to something called Christendom which, exactly like Western Science, is a social objectivity. By this I denote the fact that Western societies and individuals within them are committed to a sort of *personalism*: the view that the self-development in freedom of human personality is the highest good. In this Christendom contrasts with traditions like Islam where human flourishing is pegged more closely to the notion of a positive divine law. From this root flow a number of moral demands that characterize western societies such as freedom of worship or other rights deemed universal. Though wide in their appeal (if not universal) human rights and the secular space in which they are asserted are in their origin and essence a *theological* construction of the west. Our contemporary society is a product

---

[60]In other words, science is a social project first and foremost. Is it also 'true'? I have no doubt that it has many points of contact with the world: scientists say many true things. Yet the beliefs of Australian aborigines do as well: they also say many true things. Does one say more true things than the other? Possibly, though who has ever toted up their hits and misses? Does one speak truly on more important questions than the other? This depends on what one considers 'important'. Thinking that foraging for food in the out-backs of Australia is of prime importance would dispose you to one answer. Desiring to fly to the Moon would dispose you to another. Absent a neutral framework from which to compare the two these are not problems that admit of an empirical solution. We can all admit however that we live in a historical dispensation of which science as understood in the west is an essential component. According to this understanding theoretical integration of experience is a core value, more so than inhabiting a world saturated with narrative/affective interest. This, not knowing 'the facts' (whatever that means) accounts for our commitment to science. Why this is so, is, of course, an involved story; one involving not only the story of western science but of philosophy and religion as well. Suffice it to say that our commitment to science is a commitment to saying things that have the form of science rather than the form of myth. Perhaps we can clarify it this way: in science and, more properly, philosophy we possess the content of myth in a free reflective form. This, not the scientistic distortion that opposes logos and mythos, seems the true legacy of Greek rationalism. This is a balance it may take a new appreciation of myth to restore.

of this construction though it no longer regards it as requiring an explicit theological basis.

Needless to say, commitment to Christendom as a secular project is perfectly consistent with atheism or agnosticism especially as these take the form of Secular Humanism which is, as Nietzsche pointed out long ago, an odd sort of Christian sect.[61] However, our scientist may of course go further than this. John Doe may not only be a member of Christendom in the broad sense but may profess personal faith in Christ as his savior. Here we have something more like the stance of the western scientist and less like a general stance on the intelligibility of the world or of texts: here we are committed not just to broad principles but to a way embodied (unsurpassably) in the life of an exemplary individual. For John Doe the life of Christ has become a kind of mirror in which the face of divine love can be seen. There may be many reasons for this of a personal nature. Some may be profound and others quirky. More frequently though John Doe will center his spiritual concerns around the person of Christ because that was the tradition he was educated in and in which he has a developed habit of trust. In this he is no different from the scientist who frames all his questions about nature in terms of the tradition in which he is educated. I do note one difference however: our society offers far more alternatives to Western spirituality than it contains to western science.[62] The 'alternative' scientist can find no home in an academic institution and has little or no access to grant money or laboratory time. This though, may well be a function of the fact that science is expensive and spirituality is not. Western Science would not have the uniformity it does if anyone could do it in their basement or in a public library.

To conclude, the reader of texts, the scientist and the religious believer all walk the same tightrope. The successes of *past* interpretive acts are projected into the future; the tradition is carried forward in spite of the in-

---

[61] "It is still a metaphysical faith that underlies our faith in science- and we men of knowledge of today, we godless men and anti-metaphysicians, we, too, still derive our flame from the fire ignited by a faith millennia old, the Christian faith, which was also Plato's, that God is truth, that truth is divine." (Genealogy of Morals, 3, 24, The Gay Science, 5,344) The previous essay might be taken as my commentary on this text. Nietzsche's immediate point (which is admittedly not quite my own) is that the scientist/humanist/atheist still sets up an abstract 'truth' to which he sacrifices his will to power along with the immediacy and immanent movement of "... life, nature and history... " . (ibid.)

[62] Part of this is the perception that western science 'works': the instrumental goods we achieve through it are such that we would be fools to consider any other kind. Of course there are many ambiguities in this claim. Engineering is not a straight transcription of theory as the many engineering successes of the Greeks and Chinese attest. Plus "works at what?" is always a valid question: if solving the problem of mental illness were a criterion of success than we would probably judge Western science to be not quite the smashing success it is given out to be. For instance, it is a melancholy fact many of us have to face that anti-depressants, anti-psychotics and so on do not restore the natural chemistry of the brain but replace it: stop taking an anti-psychotic and the result is a psychotic state more severe than the one for which one was originally being treated. Confirmation bias, as Mr. Shermer himself points out, may lead us to take far more notice of signal successes than of signal failures.

evitable risk of failure. In all three cases this projection is, speaking strictly, baseless if by 'base' one means some external logical or methodological warrant or 'criterion' as the Hellenistic philosophers might have named it. Yet we are readers whether we want to be or not. The process of reading is, as noted earlier, teleological: the reader is oriented in a fundamental way towards the good, the beautiful and the true. She is oriented towards an integration and mutual enrichment of perspectives such as Dante symbolized in the heavenly circle of the philosophers. That doing this amidst the contingencies of time and place invites inevitable missteps, failures and revisions does not alter our fundamental human task as knowers and interpreters. Nor does it justify despair: there is equally no compelling reason NOT to dust oneself off and start again.[63] If I may reveal a bias by speaking Platonically, it is not evidence nor deductive logic nor inference nor induction that finally grounds our knowing and interpreting (scientific or otherwise) so much as an intuition of those highest forms (unity, beauty, truth and goodness) that underwrite whatever we can possess of knowledge on this lowly planet. We do not believe scientific theories on the basis of induction or verification and if we do then we believe in them irrationally. We believe in scientific theories as we do religions, not because 'reality' or 'observation' forces us to but because theories are figurations of order and order is an essential complement to our desire to know and our need to act. It is, in part, the internal quality of theories (their beauty or coherence in the broad sense) that claim our belief and not simply the brute realm of external fact: no straight line goes from fact to theory to belief.[64] As Plato might say they are real but imperfect images of the good (as mathematized science or *dianoia* is a real though imperfect image of dialectic or *philosophical* science). At a more directly pragmatic level they are, to quote W.V.O Quine "... a device for working a manageable structure into the flux of experience" (1205) In summation we might quote another sage: "Why do you call you me good? No one is good but God alone." (*Gospel of Mark*. 1990; 10-18) which is as much as to say that all images culminate in the intuition of what can never be imaged.

---

[63]The old alchemists never transmuted base metals into gold but most likely this was never the point. One may never attain the elixir of life but the search itself was said to be ennobling and in the process one could learn a good deal about oneself and the world around you. I find this a rather good image for the human condition as a whole.

[64]One might think correspondence to observation to be the essential thing about theories but all kinds of bad theories can be reconciled with observed facts as anyone who encounters a clever and determined flat-earther will be forced to confess. In fact there is, I have read, a theoretical model of a hollow earth (with us on the inside!) consistent with all known observations. That does not make it a whit less ridiculous.

7 WHY I AM NOT A RASTAMAN

Once many years ago on a busy street I passed some Rastafarians. In such circumstances I almost always accept pamphlets with a smile and pass on. At the time however I had a head full of Bob Marley and Burning Spear and, breaking my usual rule, attempted to engage them in conversation. It did not go well: they no more understood the questions I asked them than I understood their answers. I was a university student at the time and expecting clear, reasoned statements about what the Rastas *thought* came away with nothing. I thought at the time that no conversation was possible with people who dwelt so immediately in the poetic. I am not quite ready to let the question go however. I have since learned what it is that Rastas think. *Prima facie* it is not promising. Rastas, like mainstream Christians, believe that god has become incarnate in a human being. For them however the human in question is Haile Selassie I emperor of Ethiopia from the 1930's to the 1970's.[65] Ras Tafari is the given name of this broadly well intentioned if rather ineffective autocrat (satirized by Evelyn Waugh, rather nastily, in the novel *Black Mischief*). Rastas not only think that he is god in the flesh but that he is immortal. Haile Selassie himself insisted when asked that he was a mere man and quite mortal. (Chisholm, 1998; 175) In the 1970's he vindicated this viewpoint by, as far as anyone can tell, dying. Undeterred the Rastas have concluded that he is merely in hiding. Moreover, his imminent return will see the oppressed faithful brought back to Africa to dwell in an earthly paradise. This millennial outlook has sometimes been linked to Marxism but I find this connection tenuous. The Rastas do not dream of a universal technological society like the Marxists do but of a return to nature: their practices include (in most cases) vegetarianism, simplicity of life and the frequent consumption of cannabis as a

---

[65]Of the various assemblies of Rastas it is usually it is the house of Nyabinghi that insists most strictly on the deification of Selassie. (Edmonds, 34) We might call them 'Orthodox' Rastas if that is not stretching the term too much. Of other groups the Twelve Tribes of Israel are closer to the Christian mainstream, tending to speak of Selassie as a divine king or man of god in the broader sense while being circumspect about claiming a full incarnation. (67) The Bobo Ashanti, on the other hand, expand the list of man/deities to include their founder Emmanuel Edwards who would appear to be the second person of the Trinity (the first person being Selassie and the third Marcus Garvey). (64) Some of these differences may be social-economic as the two stricter groups tend to be rural and poor whereas Rastas from a middle class background are more liberal in doctrine and practice.

sacrament and as a natural (not technical!) panacea. (Edmonds, 2012; 48) In fact, the universal society of Western technocracy is one the Rastas see as oppressive, imperialist and corrosive of all natural values. They symbolize this society as the biblical 'Babylon' and reject it root and branch. (40) In particular they associate it with centuries of colonial oppression of African peoples. Selassie they see as an opponent of this monster and the major person to challenge it in the last century. (36) This is a bit puzzling at first: Selassie was a lifelong Ethiopian Orthodox Christian whose doctrines the Rastas can scarcely be said to share. Nonetheless they do not seem to see a problem and I have read that Bob Marley himself was baptized in the Ethiopian Church.[66] (Chisholm,175)

All of this is fatally easy for a so-called educated westerner to dismiss. I have a personal rule of thumb however. There are many 'sub-cultural' religious movements with apparently bizarre beliefs. Usually one need only listen to their songs to see what spirit is in them. The 'kingdom songs' of the Jehovah's Witnesses are unbearable treacle to my ears. The music of Scientology is risible. The music of the Rastas however immediately commands respect, both in its folk and popular forms. There is a plain but vigorous poetry to many of their songs as the music of artists like Bob Marley, Bunny Wailer and Max Romeo attests. I tend to think that anything that reaches far enough into the soul to stir genuine music and poetry almost certainly has something to be said for it: it must, surely, engage some fundamental human passion or existential concern. I must be a bit more precise however. Any cult can motivate fear or rigid obsessiveness: the frigidity and scrupulosity of Jehovah Witness theology finds its perfect counterpart in the insipid kingdom songs. There is, as Dorothy Sayers once pointed out, spiritless art: art that is about anesthetizing feeling rather than freeing it. However, there are deep and fundamental feelings liberated in art: feelings grounded in awe, in wonder, in longing, in love and anger. We can find all of these things in the songs of the Rastas and this no doubt accounts for their great and enduring popularity even among people without a religious bone in their body. In fact, many westerners seem to have a positive reaction to Rastas in general in spite of the fact that on

---

[66]The Ethiopian church has affirmed continually and no doubt with some sense of exasperation that Haile Selassie was not God. (Chisholm, 174) Being in the general ambit of Eastern Orthodoxy they could scarcely do otherwise. Nor have any of the people who knew him personally accepted the Rastafarian faith. In fact, in their treatment of theology, scripture, church history and so on the Rastas are quite cavalier. They have not attained to what scholars and theologians in the enlightenment tradition would call a critical perspective. It is fair to say that they are largely 'pre-critical' or 'non-critical' in outlook. Biblical scholars of the traditional enlightenment type would of course be aghast at this as the Rastas have even fewer critical controls over scripture and doctrine than the fundamentalists they so despise. I ask, however, that at least for the duration of this essay such people suspend their privilege: Rastas do not have the great universities of Europe or North America at their beck and call and have, until quite recently, lacked the resources to back up or develop their point of view with highly paid teachers and researchers. In fairness, they have only begun in the last few decades the kind of reflection it has taken the Christian Churches centuries to complete.

questions like sexuality their outlook is sometimes far from liberal.[67]

For this reason I am prepared to give the Rastas a fair hearing, a hearing I would not be inclined to give the chilly, sanctimonious sectarianism of certain other manifestations of Christianity. At very least they speak and understand the language of the heart. However, there is more than just aesthetics at play here. The Rastas appeal to a black Ethiopian Savior for reasons that are not themselves unsound whatever one may think of the appropriateness of deifying a man who was surely very human and very flawed. Firstly, Selassie did, as an African leader, speak up for African peoples at a time when European powers would not, or if they did, would not back up their words with actions. Moreover, his speech at the United Nations in 1963 is genuinely stirring in its call for racial harmony. It is not difficult to see how this could be interpreted as a prophetic moment for peoples of African heritage. Further, it is surely a just rebuke to European Christendom if the poor of the Caribbean cannot find their own face in the image of Christ preached in the European churches. It is surely they who have turned the face of Christ into the face of the oppressor: an image of white colonialism and bourgeois rectitude. Put these considerations together and the deification of Selassie makes a certain sense: if the white face of God is exclusive of the African and his or her concerns who then will be the black face of God? Perhaps the man who spoke, as a leader of an African nation, to their aspiration to be free and equal peoples among the nations of the world?

Then too there is ample evidence that the Rasta's depiction of Western Christendom (in its religious AND in its secular forms) as the Biblical Babylon is well founded. If the Rastas have little reason to trust Western religion they have even less reason to trust Western technocracy or the liberal economic order that underwrites it. It does not work for their interests except accidently (if at all). Even well intentioned aid agencies have made disastrous interventions in the lives of Caribbean peoples that have furthered their own power and reach but accomplished precious little else. At the same time, from the Rasta perspective, the Churches have offered heaven for their souls but only subservience for their earthly bodies. Rastas can see for themselves how these 'spiritual' people take excellent care of their mundane interests all the while preaching renunciation to those with barely anything to renounce. In such a context the desire for an earthly garden in Ethiopia has its own logic: where supernatural good has been pushed in a one sided way it is quite understandable that natural good should push back. In each case then we can see how Rasta beliefs which on their face seems bizarre are sensible when seen in the context of their general protest against their colonial oppressors.

You may, however, be wondering about the title. While I can see myself being a Rasta under dramatically altered circumstances (i.e. I can under-

---

[67]Ennis B. Edmonds discusses the problem of gender and patriarchy in Rastafarianism at some length. (Rastafari, A Very Short Introduction, 94-109) For a feminist take on this issue see "Rastawoman as Rebel: Case studies in Jamaica" in the collection Chanting Down Babylon (Imani M. Tafari-ama, 88-106)

stand why someone who leads a different life from mine would want to be one) I am not one and have no desire to be one. Perhaps this is because it seems too easy to say that truth is error flipped on its head.[68] More deeply though I must revert to what I said earlier about a critical mindset. I am quite able to separate what is legitimate in the Rasta tradition from what is spurious or silly. I am not at all sure that I could do this were I an actual Rasta for they do not seem to make these distinctions for themselves. Bizarre or manifestly spurious claims about the Bible, the history of Christianity, the culture, history and religion of Ethiopia and so on seem to have the same status with them as those beliefs with which I can readily sympathize. For instance, the Rastas often assert that Constantine or James I or some comparable villain tampered with the Christian scriptures though we have no manuscripts that show this and the Rastas offer none. (Murrell and Williams, 1998; 327) At the same time, they both use and reverence the Authorized version of the Bible: indeed, some of their doctrines and practices depend *specifically* on the KJV, such as the use of 'Jah' as short for Yaweh. (333) There are even Rastas who are convinced that Amharic was the original language of scripture! (327) Spokesmen for the movement (and they seem primarily to be men) tie themselves in knots trying to explain why God on earth was a lifelong adherent of a Church that follows all the ecumenical councils up to Chalcedon (which they reject) and recognizes as canonical the very scriptures they claim are corrupt. I am unimpressed by claims, again offered with no evidence, that Selassie secretly rejected Orthodoxy. Finally, we have all the reasons to think Selassie is dead that we have to think *any* historical figure is dead: he may well be alive but only in the sense that Napoleon or Elvis may be alive.[69] All of the above comes down to the fact that religious ideas as a form of symbolic thinking are (to a high degree) associative and that while many leaps of association are fruitful many are not.

In short the Rastas do not have a critical or reflective culture as I have come to understand it. This is in no way their fault as I indicated earlier but that does not in itself make up the deficiency. However these vices (if they are vices) are not remotely unique to them. Perhaps too, like the

---

[68]Historically at least, part of the Rasta strategy for undermining white supremacy has been inverting the values represented by the terms black and white. Where before white things were good and black things were bad, the Rastas proclaimed that black things were good and white things bad. (Murrell and Williams, "The Black Biblical Hermeneutics of Rastafari" , 333) This makes perfect sense on a psychological level: one compensates for the overvaluation of one term of a binary by emphatically asserting its contrary. However, to paraphrase Hegel, truth scorns such a trick. Inverting the values of white Europeans by elevating their opposites is a short term strategy not a final resting point and I suspect that for this reason Rastafarianism has become less and less committed to a racialist philosophy. (Barry Chavannes, "Rastafari and the Exorcism of Racism and Classism" , 62)

[69]Of course there are those who believe Elvis is alive and for reasons that seem comparable to similar beliefs about Selassie. I have a relative whose living room is a veritable shrine to Elvis Presley filled with pictures, paintings and other iconography patently religious in character. Elvis' death obviously transformed him from a flesh and blood, empirical human being to an icon. Alas, I have no explanation as to why this is so. Selassie, at least, was an actual not metaphorical king!

Mormons, they can develop a nascent culture of criticism.[70] Perhaps, as with the Jehovah's Witnesses, it is a forlorn hope. Either way once one has attained to a critical perspective it seems impossible to go back. It *does* inevitably matter to me that Haile Selassie was (like Tsar Nicholas perhaps) a decent man who was, unfortunately, raised to be a dictator and who made many missteps in governing his country. It matters very much that many of these missteps were founded in flaws in his character and that it is difficult to regard him as a saint let alone God incarnate.[71] In other words, as Selassie himself said when asked on the subject, it is dangerous in the extreme to deify a mortal man. [72] It is idle, however, to pretend that European faith communities do not struggle with the same issue. There are many Christians who still do not accept the critical study of the Bible even when practiced responsibly by sincere believers. It is easy to see why this is so. Religious symbols and images may well up from the deepest levels of consciousness (or beyond) charged with tremendous emotional and spiritual force. Traditional symbols may invoke such experiences. Eventually though they must confront ordinary reflective consciousness and here the profoundest mystic may stumble. The Ethiopian Black Christ is surely such a potent symbol for those who have been dispossessed by Western colonialism. It is surely a *legitimate* symbol. It is a symbol however that seems to crumble under the light of discursive thinking.

Thus we have a dangerous split in the human person. We have the culture of discursive rationality on the one hand without which we would quickly descend into madness; where the symbols, as Jung says, *overpower* us. On the other hand the culture of discursive reason does not offer the powerful experience of wholeness that religious symbols do and indeed is quite capable of breeding monsters of its own. We can all see how this is a

---

[70]There are signs that this is happening. We might mention, for instance, a group or 'house' called the fulfilled Rastafari who seem less eager to mythologize Selassie and much more interested in the political and social aspirations of the movement (Edmonds, 69) It is perhaps to the advantage of the Rastas that while they tend to converge on a number of common beliefs they have no creed or doctrine per se. If a particular Rasta happens to believe Selassie died there is no Bishop to excommunicate him or church council to anathematize him. Even in its most liberal iterations, however, the spirit of the Rastafarian movement is clearly sectarian. Catholicity of taste and universal curiosity are, to me at least, crucial elements of an enlightened outlook and are hardly consistent with giving over most of the globe to the Devil. What is more, being a Rasta might actually tempt one NOT to examine, say, the spirituality, art or history of Ethiopia or to ignore a great deal of what one finds there.

[71]Of course the Rastas claim that all western biographies of Selassie are tainted by Eurocentric bias. This could well be the case but how would the Rastas show this without producing a critical biography of their own?

[72]To this the Rastas respond, quite reasonably, by asking mainstream Christians why they deify Jesus of Nazaeth. I suppose many Christians would respond by asking what miracles Selassie performed and why, unlike Jesus, none of his immediate acquaintance regarded him as divine. I suppose the conversation would then proceed with each side trying to define criteria for identifying the God-man and arguing over what the historical record indicates about the personalities in question. I have my own views on this question, naturally, but I am not here to judge. I will simply note that I don't regard the result of this hypothetical discussion as foreordained: the Rasta may indeed have some hard questions for the traditional Christian as well as vice versa.

problem in our own world and not just the Caribbean.

The hard task of thinking through the implications of our faith statements cannot be shirked however and to do so would be to ignore the work generations of scholars in both the Eastern and Western traditions have done to bring the power of religious feeling together with lucidity of thought, a goal as necessary as it is elusive. While critical culture cannot sustain itself without the more primal motions of the human spirit (lest it become empty and solipsistic) it is surely not optional. Without it we lose the most crucial ability, the ability to criticize *ourselves*. I say this knowing full well that the privileged position of a western academic is a weak one from which to criticize the wretched of the earth. I don't blame or condemn anyone for whom the image of Selassie as Black Messiah is liberating and ennobling. I don't sneer at anyone who declines to participate in the critical or scientific culture of the west when they are denied the *material* benefits of that culture: benefits possessed in spades by those who hector and ridicule them. Reason is not a stick to discipline the poor. As for those who might be inclined to revolt politically can we really tell them they are not permitted to revolt mythically or symbolically as well? At the end of the day then, I can only say why I am not a Rasta and why those educated in scholarly traditions grounded in the Enlightenment cannot be Rastas: it would betray something in which *they* ought to believe. I do hope piously that *others* might come to share in these values but under the present system of global economic and political order I can scarcely demand or even expect that they do.[73] Of course, it may be that I am being unduly pessimistic even on this point. The Rastas *do* in fact have a lively tradition of discussion and debate as many observers have noted. One such observer, A.A. McFarlane, thinks it well worth asking "... whether Rasta ideas, as we have discussed them, can stand up to a searching 'Rastalike' inquiry (engaging, critical, analytic analysis)- whether in the movement, the academy, or society at large." (1998;116) I have expressed some skepticism in this article on whether this question has a positive answer. I will, however, happily be proved wrong.

---

[73]Much depends here on the fact that Rastafarianism is still very much a tradition in the making. I will note one thing however. Whether it is the Nation of Islam, the Rastas or similar groups the assumption that they are simply alien to the Western philosophical tradition is not quite true. The Rastas depend a good deal on the esoteric traditions of Europe and the Near East which ultimately transmit an imaginative and heavily mythologized Platonism. Though this would be contrary to their own self-understanding some students of the Rastas have noticed this just as I have. (A. A. McFarlane "The Epistemological Significance of I-and-I" , 119) I can draw no historical line from the world of Paracelsus, Blake and Swedenborg to the Jamaica of Garvey and Howell but the parallels, to me at least, are clear and striking. If my intuition on this is correct the Rastas may not be such strangers as seemed at first glance: McFarlane my well be on the mark in finding in them: "... a level of elenctic, intelligent discourse that would even stimulate Socrates, inter alios" . (119)

PART 2

8 PORTRAIT OF AN ISLAMOPHOBE

Tolerance for quirky and eccentric notions must like all things have its limits. Flat- Earthers are one thing but Birthers, say, are quite another: some ideas do not come from a good place and are not just absurd but pernicious. These ideas merit all the contempt that is poured on them. One of these, Islamophobia, has a surprising currency even among educated people who ought to know better. Islamophobia means fear of Islam but I am not sure the word is really apt: the form of bigotry covered by this term is not a psychological state like fear but a malign ideological construct grounded in hypocrisy, resentment and false nostalgia. This construct is now almost an article of faith among conservative Evangelical Christians. It has a considerable following among Secular Humanists as well. Thus we see that leaders of the movement include Christians like Franklin Graham and atheists like Sam Harris. So rabid are atheists and evangelicals in their hatred of Islamic civilization and culture that they seem to regard their contempt for each other as a minor obstacle to cooperation in the great struggle. Any ideology that can effect such a bizarre marriage is a powerful construct indeed.

But what is Islamophobia? Wading in the swamps of popular on-line Islamophobia (the form with the most reach and influence) we find a theory runs like this. Many modern nations have struggled with violent extremism. One could give a lengthy roll-call of organizations like the Red Brigade, the Baeder-Meinhoff Gang, the IRA, ETA, the Tamil Tigers and so on. Lately an extremist version of Islam has inspired groups like Al Qaeda and ISIL to similar acts of political terror. Since the age of revolutions at least political violence of this stripe has been a recurring problem and there are few if any who would deny that the perpetrators of it must be prosecuted to the full extent of the law. Islamophobia however is a more ambitious construction than this. Islamophobes believe themselves to have a special insight into the roots of Islamist violence: the cause of Islamist violence they contend is Islam, not just in the banal sense that, factually, it is inspired by broadly Islamic concerns but in the sense that political terror is the logical outcome of Islamic faith and that only violent Islamists are true Muslims. This claim comes in two corresponding forms depending on whether the author is Christian or secular. The first is that Islam, far from being a 'religion' is in fact a nihilistic cult of death with violence at its core.[74] The founder of this cult and inspirer of it is, one is not surprised to learn, Satan.[75] Christian Islamophobes believe that Muslim immigration to the west is part of a concerted effort to impose 'Sharia law' on the west and view all concessions to 'multi-culturalism' (in matters of dress especially) in this light. Secular Islamophobes, of course, do not invoke the prince of darkness. However, this should not delude us into thinking their position differs substantially. They have their own vocabulary for reducing Islam to a bizarre, irrational and sub-personal cult. Using biological imagery in a way that was once the province of anti-Semites they assure us that Islam is a 'mental virus' that subverts and controls the higher functions of its adherents.[76] If Muslims commit acts of terror it is because this mental virus or 'meme' is expressing its underlying nature. If Muslims *do not* commit violence this has nothing do with their religion but simply reflects the fact that, for some extraneous reason, the meme is not expressing itself. Further, if any Muslim person should *condemn* violence that is because this person is deficient in self-knowledge: anyone who truly understood the Quran would also understand their duty to kill all infidels.[77]

If one's concern is to stop violence it certainly seems counter-intuitive to tell Muslim people that their religion demands they be terrorists. It is also counterintuitive to fight extremism with harassment and discrimination which will only breed more extremism. I suspect though that the

---

[74]Here is Franklin Graham posting a Facebook response to Pope Francis on the question of Islamist violence: "Pope Francis said Wednesday that "the world is at war," but he said it was not a war of religion. I agree that the world is at war—but I disagree that it's not a war of religion. It is most certainly a war of religion. Religion is behind the violence and jihad we're seeing in Europe, the Middle East, Asia, and here in this country. It's a religion that calls for the extermination of "infidels" outside their faith, specifically Jews and Christians. It's a religion that calls on its soldiers to shout "Allahu Akbar" ("God is Great" in Arabic) as they behead, rape, and murder in the name of Islam. Radical Islamists are following the teachings of the Quran. We should call it what it is."

[75]So we are told by Megachurch Pastor, successful broadcaster and avid Trump supporter Robert Jefrees (http://www.christianpost.com/news/megachurch-pastor-robert-jeffress-paris-attacks-islam-satan-150239). I note (with astonishment) that there is an alternative account of the origins of Islam which attributes its creation to the Pope (who else!). (http://www.remnantofgod.org/PopeKoran.htm)If one is to violate all other forms of logic one might as well violate geographic logic as well.

[76]"Islam spreads like a virus. It radiates from Muslim countries that are too diseased to support it and into healthy systems that are that way because they have had the luxury of developing apart from Islam. Once in the host system, the Islam virus uses the existing machinery to make replicas of itself. Over time, the host makes unilateral concessions to the religion, feeding and appeasing it in the vain hope that this supremacist ideology can be tamed." (https://www.thereligionofpeace.com/pages/site/what-to-do.aspx).

[77]"What is not true, however, is that Islam itself is a "religion of peace." Millions upon millions of Muslims do not know or understand the basics of their faith. Countless others may comprehend it, but they choose not to exercise the inherent violence of Muhammad's seventh-century world. Even so, that does not change the basic ideals of the religion, and, like it or not, ISIS, and those of its ilk, are simply adhering to the lessons taught by the prophet in the Quran and the Hadith." (https://www.commdiginews.com/world-news/theres-no-such-thing-as-moderate-islam-only-moderate-muslims-47718/# 1ZMwkurs7hAdq50S.99).

Islamophobe relishes the thought of conflict with the hated other. Certainly this was true of the late Mr. Hitchens who nursed genocidal fantasies about the middle east to his dying day.[78] Be that as it may every plank of the Islamophobic platform is absurd on its face: the cause of Islamophobia is not Islam any more than the cause of anti-Semitism is Judaism. Firstly, and most importantly, its essentialism flies in the face of the fact that human actions are imbedded in history. Conflict between Islam and the west is not grounded in some inherent or fundamental violence of Islamic peoples (or texts) but in a history that includes imperialist rivalry, colonial domination and all the usual material factors at play in historical process. The role of Islam in this process does not differ substantially from that of any other civilization Greek, Roman, Christian or otherwise all of which have had their colonizing and empire building phases and all of which have used violence liberally to accomplish their political aims. Further, Islamist political violence in its current form may not even be a native growth: arguably the spiritual source of groups like Al Qaeda are the anti-colonialist, liberationist movements whose roots are in radical European politics. These organizations were Marxist Leninist when this was a serious alternative but are Islamist now that it is not.[79] At this point may I also remind people of the artistic, scientific, philosophical and spiritual achievements of the Islamic civilization? Is this level of achievement consistent with Satanic inspiration or mindless memetic determination? I suppose for Christians who despise all manifestations of high culture this is a tenable position. Perhaps there are secularists who are similarly philistine. My point here is that there is nothing either in the achievements or the failures of the Islamic world that cannot be paralleled in any other iteration of civilized order: in essence Muslims are as human or as inhuman as the rest of us.

---

[78] See, for starters http://original.antiwar.com/justin/2007/10/17/christopher-hitchens-and-genocide/ and http://mrzine.monthlyreview.org/2005/seymour261105.html. People I know and trust have described to me the obscene relish with which Mr. Hitchens has spoken of the effects of cluster bombs on Muslim bodies. Discourse that in any other context would be considered lunacy seems acceptable among Islamophobes. Here I will pay what may be my only compliment ever to P.Z. Myers, who had the integrity to call out Hitchens on his unhinged discourse. (http://scienceblogs.com/pharyngula/2007/10/14/ffrf-recap/)

[79] Islam like Christianity has developed a just war doctrine. (Abdel Haleem, Understanding the Qu'ran, 61-62) Like European just war theory, it insists that any war undertaken be sanctioned by legitimate authority and be conducted according to 'rules of war' which determine the treatment of prisoners and so on. On neither score do the actions of Jihadists conform to the requirements for jihad laid out by Islamic jurists. Political terror, though not unheard of in Islamic history, seems much more a European innovation. Of course the Islamophobe insists that in spite of their apparent learning the jurists do not understand Islam as well as he does and are obligated to admit the simple truth that the jihadists are right. The breathtaking hubris of this claim scarcely needs comment. One senses the Islamophobe is sometimes aware of how ridiculous this sounds and tries a different tack. Islamophobes evoke the doctrine of taqiya, the (eminently sensible) notion that in times of persecution a Moslem may conceal certain of his beliefs, as if it were a license for universal deception. Thus, Islam's religious teachers are liars rather than fools. For those curious, however, John Henry Newman has compiled an impressive list of western divines who have defended similar views on the limits of our duty to truth. (Apologia pro Vita Sua, 400-426)

Of course none of this matters to the Islamophobe who has staked his position on a kind of bad faith. The first element of this is a layer of hypocrisy so thick it smacks of projection. As I pointed out above Islamophobia is profoundly anti-historical and entails a bizarrely decontextualized account of human behavior. Islamist violence occurs as a simple consequence of Islamic belief without special motivation or context. It is well for the Islamophobe that he takes this view for anyone who looks at the context of Islamist violence will see very quickly that it is inextricably entwined with western state violence. I do not only refer here to the western funding and arming of radical Islam as a bulwark against communism in the 1980's. Nor do I refer simply to the fact that the U.S. entrusts the safety of its oil to the Wahabist Saudis whose authoritarianism serves as a hedge against democratic control of a strategic resource. I refer to the whole panoply of violence that the West inflicts so routinely on the Islamic world that we hardly register it as such. In the last few decades we have seen murderous wars in Iraq, Afghanistan, Yemen, Chechnya and Gaza either prosecuted directly by the west (including semi-western Russia) or by regional proxies. We have seen ham-fisted interventions in Libya and Syria. Thousands upon thousands of civilians have been killed in these 'humanitarian' wars and many thousands more in the chaos left in their wake. We have the routine and continuing use of drones to hunt terrorists at tremendous cost to civilian lives including those of many children. All told these Western forces have inflicted far more casualties on innocent civilians than the Islamists have.[80] Who is it again who is addicted to irrational violence? Is it the Koran that is feeding extremism or the brutality inflicted by Western security forces who use torture and humiliation on Muslim persons that they would be sickened to inflict on their own kind? Add to this the baleful legacy of colonialism (and the many atrocities that underwrote it) and the status of Muslims as an oppressed underclass in bastions of secularism and 'reason' like France and you have a toxic stew in which extremism and violence are an all too predictable result.

Of course the question remains as to why the Islamophobe adopts this bizarre position. What motivates this strange ideology which would have us in a state of permanent war with a religion of a billion people as if that were the most eminently practical proposition in the world? One might answer that it is simple racism though it is not clear (to me at least) to what degree Islam is a racialized concept. It is no secret however that Secular western elites *and* fundamentalist Christians are both insecure about the hegemony that each group once assumed to be its birthright. Consider the

---

[80] I reject the casuistry which asserts that the West is 'innocent' of these deaths because they were only 'collateral damage'. I do so even on the assumption (highly dubious) that direct terror attacks on civilians are not part of the western way of making war. Massive civilian casualties were the entirely predictable consequence of our illegal occupation of Iraq and our air and drone strikes leave individuals just as dead and families just as traumatized as terrorist attacks do. In fact, this disparity between how we view victims of 'terror' and victims of western state violence is a major sore spot in our relations with the Islamic world as politicians and journalists convey again and again the message that a Muslim life is not equivalent to a western one.

silly proposition shared by all Islamophobes that 'moderate' Muslims do not understand their own religion. What makes an angry white man on the internet with no background in Middle Eastern Studies or any knowledge of Islamic theology an instant doctor of the Koran? What makes him think that Muslim scholars are so shallow in their hermeneutic that the crudest fundamentalist style 'proof-texting' should be adequate to persuade them that they are terrorists in spite of all the religious rulings or Fatwahs to the contrary?[81] For the Islamophobe there are no reception studies: texts exist in splendid isolation from the history of their use and application concerning which no one need waste time informing himself. They mean what they mean and the rest is sophistry.

Of course it is the essence of colonial hegemony that the crudest and most unsophisticated of *us* get to define the most educated of *them* according to our categories. This just comes with our inherent superiority. The Islamophobe hates and fears that the other should define himself, that the other should act and assert autonomy rather than be the passive recipient of either his benevolence or contempt. This is why the Islamophobe pursues his peculiar ideology of reading with such tenacity. For the Islamophobe, a translation of the text of the Quran *is* the Quran and the Quran is *understood* as soon the words that compose it are deciphered. For this reason, a stock boy in Kansas and an Imam in Islamabad have before them the *exact same text* and can comment on it with equal authority: as I was told by an Islamophobic gentleman, the only thing required to read the Quran is the ability to read Arabic (though English would be a perfectly acceptable substitute given the basic equivalency of translation). From a hermeneutic point of view this is nonsense; interpretation is not just reading words on a page. It involves internalizing traditions and practices of *good* reading, dialogue with others, sensitivity to nuance, context and so on. These are *learned* skills. Thus, the text is not a static object that sits on the table with its meaning locked inside. The meaning of the text is *produced* by the cultural activity of reading which involves vastly more than an open book and a brain. Of course the Islamophobe rejects this vehemently. Where text is concerned he is an unreconstructed positivist. This is because recognizing the priority of hermeneutic process involves giving up *control of the text* to the other, who possesses the relevant linguistic/cultural background to produce good readings. This would involve the Kansas stock boy being in a position of *receptivity* to the Imam (dare one say sexual receptivity?)

---

[81]Western Islamophobes constantly harp on a selection of 'violent' texts (http://www.thereligionofpeace.com/pages/quran/violence) on the assumption that any Muslim who is 'honest' must engage in the literalistic interpretation of them favored by certain Protestant fundamentalists. They must answer to the west for their unreason by the standards of a western hermeneutic. Further, they must do so to people who know the texts in question only in translation. This kind of intellectual bullying has never struck me as either fair or plausible. Actual Quranic interpretation (Tasfir) is a complex scholarly process involving many factors and I can claim no authority on it. I have, though, learned enough about it to know that it is not the casual Sunday activity many in the west seem to think it is. One of the main planks of Islamophobia, however, is that Western characterizations of Islam are more 'objective' and 'scientific' than any possible Islamic self-understanding.

thus overturning the basic hierarchy of the world: that white people in the west instruct (penetrate?) brown people in the east and not vice versa.[82]

Thus, Islamophobia is neo-colonialism: an intellectual colonizing that is part and parcel of our physical colonizing of Iraq and Afghanistan. Indeed, as we occupy these countries and punish them with air and drone strikes the Islamophobic drum beats only louder. Our own insecurity and violence is projected onto our victims, victims we construct as existential threats *to us* even as we kill their children and poison their land. The Orientalist clichés about the opaqueness, irrationality and cruelty of the eastern other are deployed as they have always been deployed, to justify control and violence. We can now add to this stew the rancid mixture of New Atheism and Alt-Right Racism that tells us again and again that the militant verses have to be understood in their 'honest' sense and not as generations of scholars (including western scholars) have understood them. Thus we have the bizarre spectacle of 'rationalists' instructing us to read like fundamentalists not only the Bible but everything else too.

Thus the first aim of the Islamophobe is to *define* Islam and assert this definition against everything that Muslims themselves say. Indeed the Islamophobe asserts his understanding even against generations of *western* Scholarship, against 'intellectuals' who are inherently weak in will and ready traitors to their own kind.[83] The issue is not the nature of Islamic civilization as this can be understood from patient examination of its sources but his own aggrieved will.[84] None of this is to say that there are not serious gulfs of sensibility between Islam and the secular Christian and Christian west. Nor is it to say that these tensions will be easily resolved: there are

---

[82] On the 'sexualization' of the 'other' see Sartre. (341) Of course part of what we see here is an attitude also noted by Sartre: that the intuitive knowledge of the anti-semite is of another order of truth than the deracinated 'intellectual knowledge' of the Jew. No discursive thought can give the Jewish critic a glimmer of insight into a line by Racine which the least educated Frenchman can understand directly with his gut. Living from this stance of immediate truth the Kansas stock boy does not need any scholar to tell him what is in the Quran and indeed he knows that critical intelligence of any kind is only a useless encumbrance to one so blessed as he.

[83] The Islamophobe is a vehement anti-intellectual. For him to explain is to apologize and justify. Since the scholar's very business is to explain, to qualify, to understand and even to correct he is incapable of the purity of will necessary to save the west from Islamic invasion. In my experience this anti-intellectualism is usually accompanied by an almost total dependence on web pages, blogs and so on. My guess is that this is no accident: the fanatical self-certainty of the Islamophobe can find no true home in the reflective culture of print but is marvelously adapted to the immediacy of the web. As I was told recently by an Islamophobe, prosecuting the war on terror demands a 'practical' orientation and not the 'mere words' of ivory tower Academics. The connection of this stance to European philosophers of violence such as Sorel is readily apparent: at bottom, the Islamophobe would have nothing dim the clarity of his rage.

[84] Even the most stringent critic of western Orientalism Dr. Edward Said admits that many European Orientalists were men of high culture and, within the limits of their Eurocentric perspective, sympathetic observers. (178-79) By contrast he finds American discourse on Islam to be largely unburdened by scholarship or intelligence. Alas since Said wrote we have seen even further deterioration with the flourishing of an ignorant and strident 'Orientalism' on the web and elsewhere in the mass media. This quack orientalism is typified by soi-disant 'experts' like Fox news regulars Brigitte Gabriel and Steven Emerson.

core western values that do not sit easily with Islamic tradition and vice versa. I simply point out that Isamophobia will contribute nothing to their resolution and is at bottom not really intended to. Like Sartre's anti-Semite the Islamophobe is a Manichee committed to the perpetual struggle of light and dark and would commit the rest of us to the same in the face of all fact, reason and sanity.[85] As Edward Said reminds us "It is only a slight overstatement to say that Muslims and Arabs are essentially covered, discussed, apprehended, either as oil suppliers or as potential terrorists. Very little of the detail, the human density, the passion of Arab-Muslim life has entered into the awareness of even the people whose profession it is to report the Islamic world. What we have instead is a limited series of crude essentialized caricatures of the Islamic world presented in such a way as, among other things, to make that world vulnerable of military aggression." (2000;189)

To conclude, I make the following plea to Islamophobes that they reflect on the enormity of what they seem to be proposing. Western and Islamic civilization are two global facts that must come to terms with each other. Most sane people recognize this. Nowhere is this more evident than the fact that hostility, misunderstanding and contempt for the other can have no result in the end but to profoundly corrupt our own institutions and make our own freedoms less secure. Why, you might ask should I care if someone who is very identifiably not like me is detained without trial on secret evidence? Is deported to almost certain violation and torture? Is assumed to be guilty solely by association? My white skin and my Anglo-Saxon or European name surely protect me from all of that. Don't bank on it. Abuse of 'others' will inevitably leak into society as a whole. In other words, what happens if the draconian measures you propose are applied to *you*? Any government capable of suspending the civil rights of people named Fatima or Mohammed is capable in principle of suspending yours. Do not count on your white skin and European identity to protect you forever. In this, all of us, Christian, Muslim or secular are in the same boat.

---

[85]Sartre tells us "Thus, anti-Semitism is primarily Manicheanism; it explains the course of the world by the struggle between the principles of Good and Evil. There is no conceivable truce between these two principles: one of them must of necessity triumph and the other be destroyed." (338) Sartre tells us, shrewdly I think, that the Manichee's obsessive focus on evil is an easy path to self-exoneration, much easier than the intense and difficult struggle to discern and act on the good. (340) In this he resembles certain bad Christians who are more concerned with identifying (and denouncing) where the spirit isn't than with discerning where it is.

9   Dear Whites

White, I guess, is the color of my skin. I am quite happy to leave it at that but there seem to be other people who feel I should attach some special significance to my particular pigmentation. There is one group of people who want me to consider my skin color in relation to various unearned social privileges that come with it. For such people whiteness is a ticket to success not available to those who are non-white. There is another group of people however who tell me I should attach far more portentous qualities to white skin; that I should take it as a marker or token of who I am essentially as a person. Whiteness here seems to be some kind thing I should aspire to; a potentiality within me I should embrace as my inmost truth. This is something which, according to one enthusiast, makes me an 'explorer and conqueror' (two things I should apparently aspire to be) and a 'child of the sun' (sic).[86] It seems that whiteness is here doing duty for an older concept 'soul' which is in fact far different (more on this below!). This 'white essence' inclines me to noble, perhaps heroic attributes. One inevitable corollary of this seems to be that having another essence would incline me to other character traits less admirable. If 'whiteness' makes me a conqueror, then presumably 'blackness' would make me something less than a conqueror. At any rate such people seem to think that this 'white essence' is something I should take some particular pride in, so much so that it is a special crime to mingle it with any other.

I think I understand what the first group of people are saying tolerably well. Of the second I have to confess I haven't a clue what they could be talking about. This is why the following essay is addressed to white people, particularly those we might call 'white supremacists' or 'white nationalists'. I expect no person of color to waste their time with this discussion. This is an in-house matter for white people and that is why I will craft arguments for things that need no argument outside our own confined circle. So, dear 'whites' before I reject or accept your point of view I make the simple, humble request that you explain it to me. To help you I will lay out my

---

[86] Mr. Richard Spencer has delivered himself of a stirring speech upon the occasion of Trump's election. It is to this that I refer. I am told that Mr. Spencer is regarded as a 'leading intellectual' among the so called Alt Right. Video footage of Mr. Spencer's speech is available at https://www.youtube.com/watch?v=1o6-bi3jlxk& t=108s. What kind of intellectual Mr. Spencer is others may judge, I note though that he has advanced academically all the way to a doctoral program which he did not complete.

76

concerns about 'whiteness' and why I seriously doubt it is a thing that
exists (or that it is a thing I should give a fig for even if it does exist). So,
I will lay out my thoughts on the subject so you can enlighten me. Please
note though that this is a philosophic criticism and I pretend to no special
knowledge of genetics or any other relevant science. These sciences (as
currently understood) create serious problems for your position but that
can a be a discussion for another day.[87]

On a superficial level I notice that whiteness seems unrelated to skin
color. There are white people (such as Jews) who are not said (by you)
to possess any of the heroic qualities of whiteness. This also used to be
said of the Irish, who, though 'white' on the outside, were once thought to
be inwardly 'black'.[88] To use biological terms, whiteness is not a pheno-
type. I assume then that if I dyed myself purple this would not affect my
whiteness in the least bit. I assume too that since phrenology is no longer
a science whiteness is not a function of my cranium either. At any rate I
notice that Hispanics (Cervantes and the golden age of Spanish literature
notwithstanding) are not 'white' (according to you) and I challenge anyone
to tell a Hispanic skull from mine.[89] I am left to conclude whiteness has
to do with something more fundamental and the most logical candidate
for this fundamental thing would seem to be D.N.A. Some of you speak of
'blood' when this question comes up but I can only think you mean it as
a metaphor. It is a funny thing though that time and place seem to determine the boundaries of whiteness far more than biology. Today's white is
yesterday's non-white (as in the case of the Irish) and today's non-white is
yesterday's white (as in the case of supposedly *Caucasian* Spanish speak-
ers). You will not like to hear it but this strongly suggests to me that

[87]The basic problem is that the science of taxonomy has shifted to a genetic basis.
When applied to the human species this new taxonomy does not map onto the old divi-
sions between negroid, mongoloid, caucasoid and so on. In other words, race as racialism
has traditionally understood it is not a currently recognized biological phenomenon. This
makes race primarily a cultural phenomenon and then it is difficult to see why it should
have the immutability racialists claim. Mr. Shermer gives a good account of this problem in Chapter 15 of his book (242-251) Afrocentric versions of racialism, based on the
supposed virtues of melanin are equally problematic. Indeed, so bizarre are the assertions made by the 'melanin theorists' I have so far encountered that I cannot dismiss the
possibility that they are spoofs. Be that as it may my objections apply in the same way
to those who fetishize 'blackness' though it remains perfectly understandable that those
who have been forced into the latter category would attempt an ironic reversal of values
by elevating the subordinate term of standard racial binaries.

[88]As Henry Bracken notes: 'L. Perry Curtis notes, Apes and Angels shows how exten-
sive the effort was to assimilate the Irish to the simian or the black- the black's inferior
status having already been scientifically established." ("Essence, Accident and Race"
1981: 267). Bracken notes the role of Lockean empiricism in naturalizing human intelligence as a key factor in the rise of modern racism. His follower Hume took this theme up
with gusto as undersecretary of state delivering himself of many patronizing comments
on 'negroes' and 'Irishmen'. (259)

[89]Does the presumed admixture of indigenous 'blood' plays some role here? I find it
hard to say. However, as the Mayans and Aztecs produced complex civilizations I can
only assume that their 'blood' was of fairly good quality too. This seems one instance
where linguistic bigotry has gotten mixed up with the racial kind in a pre-reflective and
incoherent way.

Marxists (and others) who claim 'race' is not a natural phenomenon at all but a social construct that changes with the shifting needs of power and privilege may be spot on.

However, I notice as well that whiteness has the status of a moral quality in some circumstances. For instance, I can fail at being white, particularly if I am being hoodwinked into believing in the equality of the other 'races'. Whiteness, then, is like a talent I bury in the sand or a muscle I fail to exercise. It seems odd to say of my genetic code, however, that I fail to exercise it. I suppose though that something like the following may be true: perhaps 'white' DNA predisposes us statistically to certain traits which it is up to us to develop. But then notice what happens: my success as an individual then becomes the product of my choices and it is hard to see why I should be praised for or take pride in my particular genotype. An artist may benefit from having 20/20 vision but we praise her for her work not her eyesight. Further, if indeed black people or others lack predispositions to certain valuable traits (a thing I GRAVELY doubt) that does not mean they can't compensate for this through hard work, education or ambition: Cezanne was a great artist without being a great talent.[90] Again it seems to be not blackness or whiteness that matters but how one conducts one's life. Even if I granted everything you say about race, character, intelligence and so on that would mean only that whites are *luckier*. It would not imply that whites as a whole or indeed any given white person was therefore *better*. It is not to anyone's credit that an oil patch happens to be on their land as opposed to a neighbor's.[91]

Inevitably we are faced here with the is/ought distinction. Insofar as whiteness is some natural state it is impossible to see why it is anything but morally neutral. White pride, then, seems like an oxymoron as whiteness is not a thing one can take legitimate pride in any more than acute hearing or big bones. So, I am again at a complete loss as to why I or anyone should invest any mystical properties in being white. Perhaps, though, I misunderstand my white brethren. Maybe when they speak of whiteness they mean something cultural not something natural. Perhaps they refer to the glories of European civilization and say that THAT is something I should take pride in. To be frank, it has never occurred to me even once that I should take pride in the accomplishments of Bach for the simple reason that they are his not mine. I suppose this might be otherwise if the greatness of Bach was a function of a certain genotype we both shared but

---

[90]Every teacher and professor knows that students who apply themselves can make much better progress than students who don't even though the latter surpass them in natural gifts.

[91]White supremacists who consider themselves Christian should meditate upon the following text: "And think not to say within yourselves, we have Abraham to our father: for I say unto you, that God is able of these stones to raise up children unto Abraham." (Matthew, 3-9) White nationalists who reject Christianity are far more consistent in their views though what remains of the glory of European 'art and architecture' (so fondly evoked by Mr. Spencer) when Christianity is effaced is difficult to say. Perhaps it consists of Also Sprach Zarathustra or (maybe) the rings and bracelets found in Viking funeral boats.

even then it was Bach who wrote the *Art of Fugue* not some blob of genetic goo (let alone the pigmentation of his skin) and I, white as I am, could never do the like.[92] Thus, *even if* European civilization were demonstrably superior to, say, the civilization of China it is hard to see how any of this redounds to my particular credit. It is hard to see why *I* should be proud of a fact over which I have no control.[93] Again, the object of pride is the work accomplished not the natural dispositions of the worker which can be easily, and tragically, squandered. However, if this is what you proud whites really think then any person of any race could become whiter simply by becoming more European in outlook and culture (perhaps by developing a taste for single malt or caviar). If you are not prepared to admit this, then your position falls into the incoherence pointed to above: you reduce cultural phenomena to their natural substrate and confuse the 'is' with the 'ought'.

At any rate I appreciate European culture as much as anyone and I notice that you say certain things that do not (to say the least) seem a comfortable fit with the civilization you claim to admire. Let me bring your attention to a white man named Rene Descartes. In a book called the *Discourse on Method* he says the following: "... the power of forming a good judgment and of distinguishing the true from the false, which is properly speaking called good sense or reason, is by nature equal in all men." (1969;107) What he means by this is that mind insofar as it is mind functions the same way in all its instances. There may be developed or

---

[92] At any rate I would have thought that the appropriate response to the genius of Bach or Milton or Dante would be humility not pride. Certainly I cannot bask in the glory they have earned simply on the basis of my skin color. Indeed, it is beyond bizarre to assert that reading Shakespeare is instrumental to contemplating and appreciating some larger thing called whiteness, as if he were the mere expression of some primordial racial genius and not an individual creator in his own right. 'Whiteness' has never written a play or sung a song.

[93] This causes me to suspect that 'white pride' is really some form of compensation for an underlying insecurity or anxiety. Part of this I suppose has to do with anxiety over social status among downwardly mobile whites or whites who, while still reasonably prosperous, live in fear of downward mobility. However, listening to what White Nationalists say I am struck by one thing. There is the persistent sentiment among them that along the critique of racism comes an accusation of inexpungable collective guilt. White Nationalists think their anti-racist critics are asking them to submit to a permanent moral tutelage and that guilt is being used as a lever to manipulate their consciences. They then react with a defensive (and as we have seen incoherent) assertion of their 'compromised' white identity. It is of course a fact that guilt often is used this way in human relationships (as an expression of the will to dominate). Activists in the progressive community, naturally, do not see themselves doing so. They see this defensive assertion of whiteness as yet more proof that racists are hopelessly vitiated and corrupt. It is true that few people (if any) are intentionally or consciously using guilt in this manner: hardly anyone can see themselves acting in such a fashion. A fish however cannot see water. How we see ourselves rarely corresponds to how we come across to others. To diagnose and overcome the dangers of such mutually reinforcing negative interactions both groups need to consider the dialectic of sin and grace in St. Paul who, along with Anselm of Canterbury, is history's great teacher on this problem. There are grave dangers in the general occlusion of the theological tradition one of which is complete loss of insight into a central problem of our time: how to impute guilt with love and how to accept guilt without shame (a very different concept!).

undeveloped minds but mind as such provides us all with the same power of judgment and it is up to us to exercise this well or ill. Since it is as obvious as can be that white skinned humans are not alone in possessing minds (the Great Wall of China *not* being a monumental accident) it is obvious that all possess the same basic power of discerning good from evil and true from false.[94] We all then have the same *potential* though particular individuals can judge or reason poorly from sloth, fatigue, lack of education or debilitating illness. If I do so this is not a problem with my mind but a problem with the circumstances in which my mind is attempting to operate. Cartesian 'reason' then is like the soul in Plato or the agent intellect in Aristotle. It is indifferent to its human substrate, operating in bodies both male and female, black and white. Indeed, there is some evidence it may operate in the higher mammals as well as in humans. Almost certainly, intelligent life forms on other planets who have mind will not have human bodies like ours. For Descartes, mind does not even need a body as angels and God possess intelligence far greater than ours. Thus, as Braken notes: "... if one is a Cartesian, a defender of mind/body dualism, it becomes impossible to state a racist position." (1981;260)[95]

As a number of you profess to be Christians I draw your attention to the fact it is a widespread belief among Christians that the core or essence of the human person includes an immortal soul and that the great Christian thinkers such as Augustine and Aquinas expound the nature of this soul much as Plato and Aristotle do. Descartes, of course, stands in this tradition as well.[96] Cartesian mind also looks forward to the autonomous moral agent of Kant and the free subject that underlies the liberal/contractual

---

[94] Hath not a Jew eyes? Not one of the basic interests or passions of human beings are 'white'. Religion, art, song, sport, philosophy and science have existed in all parts of the globe and in all known phases of civilization. Even if I think Europeans are the 'best' at all these things the notion that all the rest are thereby clumsy or crude or mindless is surely ridiculous. Nor does it mean that Europeans owe their 'success' in these endeavors to any intrinsic physical superiority (as opposed, say, to historical luck).

[95] Of course it is still possible for a Cartesian to be a racist in his personal affairs. Conversely an empiricist can be an anti-racist in his conduct. Bracken is concerned only with the history of intellectual justifications of racism and even these can be as contingently historical as they are logical. (263) Nonetheless certain philosophical positions supply more scope for asserting absolute natural differences between humans than others. Certain of these seem typical of early modernity such as Lockean skepticism about substance(261). Thus, while racism is a necessary falsehood for any Cartesian who understands his own principles it is for a Lockean only a contingent one. It is perhaps insufficiently noted (by racists AND by their critics) how modern the concept of race is. It is scarcely noticeable in the medieval period where identities tended to focus much more on religion or social caste. Alas, even some on the left treat 'whiteness' as an immutable category blithely referring to figures like Plato or St. Augustine as 'white'. However, there can be no white people without the concept of whiteness and that concept appears to be strictly modern.

[96] Consider for instance the following passage from St. Paul: "For ye are all children of God by faith in Christ Jesus. For as many of you as have been baptized into Christ have put on Christ. There is neither Jew nor Greek, there is neither bond nor free, there is neither male nor female: for ye are all one in Christ Jesus." (Galatians,3, 26-29) As is apparent from Augustine and his successors this inwardness of Christian faith (indifferent to race and sex as Paul says here) has blended with the 'soul' of classical philosophy as a crucial moment in the founding of the modern subject.

80

tradition of Locke and his successors. All these positions assume a non-naturalist (ie. autonomous and self-determining rather than heteronomous or mechanical) account of subjectivity however differently they may articulate this belief.[97] They also underlie the moral and political institutions of the modern west insofar as they have been morally progressive as opposed to rapacious and exploitive.[98] Here I will be very blunt. Remove Plato, Aristotle, Descartes, Kant and their successors from the European tradition and I have to say I don't especially admire it. Replace soul, mind, and freedom with the crude naturalism of skin color, blood and protein strings and I will say to you what is only true: that India, Africa and the Islamic world will be the vanguard of civilization not us 'whites'. If all we have to offer the world is a naturalism cruder than any materialist has yet dreamed of (all backed up with a gutter interpretation of Darwin) then the 'white genocide' you fear can't happen fast enough. I have taught students from Africa imbued with a wonderful philosophic and ethical spirit and I will be happy to leave civilization in their capable non-white hands.

---

[97] Of course how the self-legislating, self-thinking subject of modern philosophy is related to the determinism of nature is a vexed question on which philosophers divide even today. I have my own intuitions on the matter which I shall discuss elsewhere. At this point though it occurs to me that if racism is indeed a rational truth then every rational being should be capable of recognizing this. However, no rational agent can regard himself as intrinsically inferior to any other. Racial prejudice cannot be universalized and if we are seriously committed to it entails rejecting reason in its practical form.

[98] Alas I fear that it is precisely exploitation and rapacity that many of my interlocutors admire. After all, they inform me that 'crusading and conquering' are the marvelous gift of my white blood. If this is so, however, I must say that I admire the Assyrian civilization far more than our own as their imperialism was unencumbered by any tendency to critical reflection. Anyway, as some future (or indeed alien) race will, no doubt, far surpass us in these qualities I see no grounds for being overly concerned about white conquerors and crusaders in particular.

10 Violence: An Idea whose Time has Gone?

In Western European culture there are two profound considerations of violence: that of the Greeks and that of the Hebrews. One is realist one is idealist. There is a profound consideration of violence in the Eastern tradition as well in the *Gita* and in the teachings of Siddartha. It seems to break down on similar lines. In China, Mohists and others debated the utility or lack thereof of violence. I am sure there are other considerations in traditions unfamiliar to me. At any rate our options, whether in the east or the west or elsewhere are two: to deify war or to end it. For the Greeks war is a god as strife is held in eternal balance with love. This god is destructive, irrational, and exacts a heavy price from his worshippers. This god wills violence for its own sake whatever the cause. Yet, he is part and parcel of the order of things, a member of the pantheon and though loathed by the other gods he cannot be wished away. His visitations are to be feared but ultimately accepted. This understanding of violence is given paradigmatic expression in Homer's description of the shield of Achilles.[99] Contrast this to the account of the Hebrew prophets. For Isaiah and his fellow prophets, the messianic kingdom will usher in the age of peace: "He shall judge between the nations, and impose terms on many people: they shall beat their swords into plowshares, and their spears into pruning hooks: one nation shall not raise the sword against another, nor shall they learn train for war again" . (*Isaiah* 1990 2,4) War is not an intrinsic part of the world: it is not ontological like gravity. It is a temporal (not eternal) result of the fallen nature of humans. The end times then will usher in an age in which 'swords are beaten into ploughshares' and violent conflict will cease. It is not my aim here to settle a difference so profound. All I want to suggest in

---

[99]Naturally, attitudes to war vary in Antiquity. In both Greece and Rome war was an arena in which a man pursued excellence and fame. Yet at the same time we find an attitude of ironic detachment towards it in Horace as well as the studied indifference of Lucretius. In the plays of Euripides, we find the horrors of war milked for pathos. In Sappho's famous lyric we find the whole heroic panoply of the epic tradition rejected for the pursuit of erotic fulfillment. However, it is hard to say whether in all this we can discern principled pacifism. Still, the most powerful image of the futility of war is given us by Aeschylus: in the sacrifice of Iphigeneia we see that the true price of destroying the other is the destruction of our own. Much of what I have to say below is a mere footnote to the tragedian's insight.

the following is that we live in a unique period of history. We live in a time when ending organized violence altogether seems at least thinkable. Why? Because the data is in. We have an immense tradition of warfare and other forms of violence stretching back to the dawn of recorded history. We can understand the dynamics that lead to warfare and understand the ways in which violence has been dramatically oversold as a method of problem solving. We understand the rhetoric of war and the way it is almost always at odds with truth. We can legitimately ask whether there is any problem to which war or other forms of organized violence is a long term solution. Further, more thought has been given to non-violent forms of resistance than at any point in the past. This puts us in a unique position to ask a fundamental question about the human condition: is organized violence an intrinsic or accidental part of it?

I will take a somewhat roundabout route to addressing this question. One might begin with the notion that violence is a tool in a toolbox, like flattery, bribery or persuasion. Certain people of a Marxist bent seem to take this view. For this view violence is simply one more way of effecting desired changes to be regarded exactly as any of the others. Such people fall into the Leninist 'the end justifies the means' camp. I will begin my consideration by dissenting from this view. Violence is a prima facie harm. This is so in the obvious sense that the object of violence is harmed physically and psychologically sometimes to an extreme degree. The victim of violence also suffers the moral harm of being reduced to a thing, an object to be manipulated by force rather than reasoned with. However, we must also note that the harm of violence falls equally on the perpetrator. The subject of violence suffers moral and psychological harm exactly as the victim does, perhaps more so as the harm can be more implicit and therefore more insidious. Further, even witnesses of violence can suffer psychological trauma such as jurors in a trial. Violence, clearly, places a great strain on the human psyche as well as its more direct effects on the body. For pacifists these harms are so great that they reject violence altogether. I am not quite ready to jump to this conclusion however for reasons I will state below. Yet I think it is minimally clear that the harms of violence are significant enough that any proposal to engage in violence should meet a high bar of skepticism. If one risks bodily harm, desensitization and trauma for oneself and others then one should have a very compelling reason for doing so. There are some obvious constraints: given the *prima facie* harms I have outlined violence cannot be resorted to when there are alternatives which do not entail inflicting these or similar harms. Violence, again minimally, is a tool of last resort. It may turn out in fact that there are, in all instances, better alternatives to lethal force but we will consider this below.

Philosophers have laid out a number of other criteria for determining when violence is justified. Collectively these have come to be labeled Just War Theory.[100] Let me begin by considering one of these: that of authority.

---

[100] Just War Theory is expressed in various ways some involving more principles and others involving fewer. For the sake of simplicity, I will focus on authority, proportionality, and likelihood of success as basic criteria. The form of Pacifism considered here is

Any war is justified if and only if it is officially declared by properly constituted authority and overseen by the same. In effect, there are no private wars and no private armies. The reason is obvious if considered in consequentialist terms. If any private person (say a terrorist) can wage his own personal war against any other nation no genuine state of peace between nations can ever exist. The same is true in civic terms: if any private citizen can wage war against his or her own government then there is literally no state of civic peace.[101] Anyone who plants a bomb on a train for his cause sanctions anyone else to do the same for theirs with results as dire as they are predictable. Even in the case of tyrannical governments any opposition force must show some evidence of broad-based democratic support before becoming a legitimate army. As the situation in Syria exemplifies a hodgepodge of militias representing various dueling class and ethnic interests has neither the right nor even the ability to make war. If, as claimed above, violence is a prima facie harm and peace a prima facie good the business of war making cannot be left to just anyone. War must be made in the name of some person or body to whom the war makers answer. This is especially true as soldiers have to be accountable for their actions particularly if there is a question of incompetence, atrocities or acts of poor discipline such as looting or needless vandalism. Thus, we may say in general that no war can be waged outside a clear structure of accountability of which a parliament or international body like the U.N. would be examples. There is, moreover, a concern I should register here: given a strong Kantian position that persons are objects of unconditional respect (ends in themselves) it may well be questioned whether *anyone* has the authority to order the death of human beings. Many people accept this argument with respect to capital punishment but is the case of war any different? We must keep open the question of whether there are, *de facto*, such authorities as just war theory requires.

Another criterion of just war concerns proportionality. A war is just if and only if the evils it seeks to remedy are greater than the evils suffered from the war itself. This of course is not an easy balance to calculate. What does the right to self-determination of the Falkland Islanders weigh when balanced against the British and Argentine expenditure in lives and money (anything spent on a war is not spent on schools and hospitals)? From the other side what is sovereignty over the Malvinas worth when

the minimal form that rejects the use of lethal force. Again, for brevity's sake, I will not be considering the morality of non-lethal acts of violence though it is a legitimate and indeed important question.

[101] By civic peace I mean a state in which the ordinary intercourse of life is not disrupted by the threat or actuality of large scale violence. I distinguish it from eschatological peace which is the peace of a fully realized kingdom of ends. Thus, civic peace is consistent with private acts of violence, misbehavior by public officials and indeed with all the oppressions and miseries of life. Civic peace is a negative limiting condition that does not add open warfare to the ordinary unhappiness of the world. As such it is a real but partial good that we should not forego lightly even as we work towards eschatological peace as a comprehensive good. Thus, I am no fan of that well known graffito according to which everything outside of eschatological peace is a state of war: all that is short of heaven is not therefore hell.

weighed against the same? What sort of goods are proportional to the destruction of human beings who are unconditional ends? Further there are many incidental harms that last far beyond the conflict itself including generational trauma for the families of dead or maimed as well as damage to the environment. This later is of particular concern today as armed conflict currently leaves behind appalling and dangerous litter such as land-mines, unexploded cluster bombs, depleted uranium shell casings as well as leakage of the many fuels and toxic chemicals employed by modern militaries. This kind of damage unfolds over generations and is thus extremely difficult to calculate. A further consequence is that war, and particularly the rhetoric of war, pollutes the moral environment. It brings with it jingoism, sham patriotism, demonization of the enemy, egregious assaults on truth and dubious moral shortcuts that make atrocious behavior even to those on our own side slowly but surely more acceptable. Moral lines that are firm in peace are erased in war such that brutalization of our own combatants becomes as routine as brutalization of the enemy.

That said there may indeed be threats to the existence of nations or peoples so grave that these evils are supportable: this has yet to be determined. My immediate point is that we need a more nuanced concept of the harms of war than has traditionally been the case in discussions of proportionality. We need to measure the consequences of the loss of peace in all their dimensions before saying that any proposed act of violence is proportional in the goods it achieves. Above all we cannot be naïve about the moral effects of violence on the agent who wields it. I have talked to a number of people who seem perfectly convinced that violence is a tool that can safely be wielded by the pure at heart, whether these be 'honest patriots', 'good guys with a gun' or 'social justice warriors'. No one is fit to wield violence who is ignorant of the danger it presents his own soul. Those who believe they cannot be corrupted by it will be those who fall first and fall deepest. It is sobering to realize that armies, all armies, tend to act in the same ways whether they are communist, capitalist, fascist or other. For instance, they frequently use the chaos of war as an opportunity for looting and rape, the latter often on a grotesque scale.[102]

Indeed, achieving goods is essential. According to Just War Theory any war is just if and only if it has some reasonable prospect of success. No goods are achieved by conflicts which are futile. As any war must achieve some good such wars can have no justification. Nor can these goods be accidental (like the invention of feminine hygiene products in WW1). They have to bear a clear relation to the stated aims of the conflict. This of course means that a war needs some clearly stated aim. The aims of the

---

[102] As corollary of this no war can be prosecuted using means that are as unjust as the evils the war is seeking to redress. A genocide cannot be met with a counter genocide. Indiscriminate aerial attacks on civilians cannot be me by more of the same. Of course the tendency in war is to use whatever force will get the quickest cheapest result. Also, there is the natural inclination to pay back the enemy in his own coin. In WW2 this meant the slaughter of civilians in cities like Hamburg and Dresden as well as the mass rape of German women and girls by the advancing Red Army (an atrocity incited by Stalin himself). Thus, a war is just if and only if it is prosecuted by just means.

conflict cannot be subject to constant ad hoc adjustment (a favorite trick of politicians mired in unproductive warfare). Thus the means proposed must be such as to offer a reasonable prospect of attaining the ends. In spite of the romantic allure of noble last stands it was probably correct of the Danish government not to oppose the German occupation with conventional forces. In spite of the romantic allure of the partisan it was probably pointless to risk so many lives resisting the Nazis with guerilla tactics when this activity had so little effect on the outcome of the war.[103] I say probably because these are not always easy calculations to make[104]. One might legitimately wonder however whether the intrinsic vagueness of 'ends' bedevils any attempt to apply this criterion. The ultimate aim of any war is a just peace and it is questionable whether five millennia of organized violence have achieved this in any lasting form. It is questionable how often it has achieved this even in temporary form. One might, if one is a foreign policy realist, state that the ultimate aim of wars is the 'national' interest. Usually though this translates into narrow class and commercial interests. How often have farmers and tradesmen had any real stake in the conflicts they are conscripted to fight in? Even if one gives a broader and more generous definition of this phrase however the ambivalence remains. Though every war seems absolutely necessary to those who wish to wage it how many nations can be said to have achieved their aims or interests in any stable form through armed conflict? As one striking example consider the defeat of Nazism by the allies in WW2. No nation has ever been crushed with violence on the scale of that inflicted on Germany. Nazism was defeated as thoroughly and completely as any movement could be defeated. Yet here we are not even a century later faced with resurgent right wing Fascist movements. One is also reminded of the interminable wars of antiquity which bought barely a century of the *Pax Romana*. It is sobering to think that, as Conrad Brunk reminds us, the theoretical ceiling for the success rate of violent conflict is % 50.[105] (2005; 584)

---

[103] While the resistance was useful at auxiliary tasks like intelligence gathering it was never a threat to any German occupation. The Germans were defeated a. by massive and costly land battles in the east and b. by the American air campaign in the first half of 1944 which crippled the Luftwaffe as an effective fighting force. In the east and in the Balkans partisans were a useful adjunct to conventional forces but they contributed nothing at all to the root cause of the allied victory the west: total air dominance achieved over France and Germany. I say this because the French Resistance is one of our paradigms of 'good violence' whose brave activities contributed to our 'final victory'. Like paradigms in science, paradigms in violence teach us which examples to follow or not follow (be Churchill not Chamberlain!) in order to attain which ends. Many of these deep cultural scripts (in which our turn to violence invokes the narrative crisis which brings about the resolution of the plot) crumble on exposure to reality which is why we try as much as possible not to examine them.

[104] Of course in the strict sense they are not 'calculations' at all but matters of prudential judgment. There is no 'formula' for using these criteria any more than there is for any other species of ethical judgment.

[105] As Trudy Govier notes: "A major problem with our thinking about violence is the highly unrealistic nature of our expectations about what it can accomplish. Among the many sources of unreflective thinking in this area is the fact that our expectations arise from fictional narrative more than from real experience." (548) Another is confirmation

And herein lies the main problem I wish to address. It should be plain already that examples of conflicts that fulfill all or any of the criteria laid out above are extremely rare (if they exist at all). Wars outnumber just wars by a very large margin: such a large margin that we might legitimately wonder what makes them so popular. Of course this point cuts both ways. It can be used by pacifists to argue that wars should not occur. At the same time, it can be used by realists to argue that any attempt to apply moral judgment to war is futile. Still, I think I have established that there are vastly more wars than there are good wars whether we are using a moral standard or even simply a pragmatic one. One might argue however that since war is such a frequent occurrence it must have some value of some kind. I would answer yes but remember that for just war theory the aims of conflict must be intrinsic not accidental. It is clear that sword makers prosper if swords are in demand. It is clear that officers who seek promotion and personal fame also benefit from war. It is also clear that anyone who has an army has a strong incentive to use it as equipment and tactics get tested in combat and the army gains a cadre of combat tested veterans (a huge edge in future conflicts). The *Luftwaffe* for instance gained enormously from the conflict in Spain while the Japanese air and land forces both benefited from constant warfare in China. Taken together these ulterior motives (and others like them) go a certain way to explaining our readiness to resort to warfare.

However, I think that invoking things like profiteering barely scratches the surface of our addiction to warfare. To conclude this brief analysis, I want to point to two psychological mechanisms that function in turning war from a possibility into an inevitability: escalation and threat inflation. Many wars are a product of a process of escalation whereby the failure of modest uses of force to effect change is taken not as a problem with force itself but simply with the amount applied. Other wars are a product of the psychological process by which particular threats are generalized into a mood of existential menace that justifies any response no matter how extreme or apparently futile. The first is a version of the gambler's impulse to double down on his bet. Having committed ourselves to some violence we thereby commit ourselves to more and more rather as a small lie grows into

---

bias. We tend to retain in our minds successful or putatively successful instances of violent action and generalize from these. We forget that by definition at least half of all wars must fail and that the number only falls from there. War has not improved Iraq or Afghanistan or made western nations more secure from terrorism. War did solve the problem of rivalry between the European nation states (for now) but only at obscene physical and moral cost. Millennia of ancient warfare produced barely a century of general peace. In the annals of warfare, we find blood and money squandered in inconclusive campaigns, we find transient victories turning into deeper defeats, we find sophisticated people like the Athenians whipping themselves into a militaristic frenzy only to hurtle off a cliff (literally in this case). Even in successful wars like the Civil War we find the victors winning the battles but losing the peace: America is the same divided nation it began as. For every 'success' we can point to dozens of failures. Why do we think that what has failed so often (either fully or in part) will work this time? At any rate if the assumption is that the aim of war is peace then it has been a signal failure.

a big lie. WW1 is an example of how nations can find themselves involved in levels of violence grotesquely disproportionate to anyone's actual stake in the conflict. A sacrifice committed must be redeemed by greater and greater sacrifice as the psychological pain of admitting it was wasted is too painful. I suppose this is a version of the good money after bad phenomenon. The basic problem is that violence has no predictable result. The enemy may wilt before our show of force, as we confidently expect him to, but many a general has failed on the battlefield due to the perverse will of the enemy, who does what he wants to do rather than what he is expected to do (as the adage says a plan that assumes a passive enemy is no plan at all). The enemy may well respond to force with force thus creating a situation where we must escalate or withdraw. Escalation, alas, draws us into a conflict far more involved and costly than any we intended. We quickly find ourselves dragged deeper and deeper into a conflict that renders fewer and fewer rewards in relation to ever spiraling costs.[106]

The second process is one where 'mere' threats are elevated into existential threats and particular threats become universal. There is a tendency to regard every conflict as part of an epic struggle for survival. This is the result of applying a Hobbesian logic to the world. Every free nation in the world is a threat to any other, at least in principle. Every human is a threat to any other in the same sense. Now of course nations and persons *do* face threats of a specific and limited kind. Notice though how the inflationary rhetoric of war shapes our perception of these threats. Threats come from a specific kind of person, the capital E enemy. The capital E enemy has no understanding of reason and no reasonable motives or comprehensible demands. Force, though, is a language he is said to understand and respect. The enemy with a capital E must never be appeased. Any show of reason or compromise towards him will be taken as a sign of weakness and an opportunity for him to escalate his demands. Further, we cannot sit around waiting for him to attack us. Indeed, the wiser course is to hit him before he hits us. War with the capital E enemy is inevitable, only a matter of who fires the first shot. Certainly he will make no effort to avoid it and it would be foolish to allow him the advantage of striking the first blow. Finally, this enemy is Adolf Hitler: we cannot repeat history by letting this enemy grow in power and ambition for this is what the European nations did in the thirties and this resulted in the holocaust. Sometimes, and the fevered mind of Hitler may stand as an example, the enemy is omnipresent and the wars of the nation are part of an eternal struggle for survival in which we must conquer or perish. Are there capital E enemies in the world?

---

[106]This is especially true of the modern logic of total war. As C.S. Lewis once pointed out there is a price to be paid for regarding war as a moral activity: every war then becomes a crusade. (48) If every conflict is framed in absolute moral terms, then no conflict can be resolved short of total victory. The goal becomes the elimination of the enemy. Escalation is built into the very nature of total war along with an ever expanding list of valid targets. Thus we see in the twentieth century the move from attacking soldiers to attacking national infrastructure to killing civilian workers to, finally, the environmental terrorism of nuclear tipped ICBM's. Each of these moves is a necessary step towards ending not the war but the enemy and the evil for which he stands.

Perhaps but that is irrelevant. The inflationary rhetoric of war constructs a capital E enemy whether one exists or not. All enemies must be treated as Hitler should have been treated and any people who fails to see this paves the way for its own destruction.[107]

Consider then the obstacles that must be overcome by anyone who proposes violence as a course of action. This person must indicate an authority competent to declare war. They must show that the evils to be prevented by war are greater than the costs of waging it. They must show that the objects of the war are achievable by the actions proposed and only by the actions proposed. Further, anyone who proposes violence must ask himself whether he is proposing it because he is trapped in a cycle of escalation that it is in his best interest to escape. Moreover, he must ask himself honestly whether he has inflated a finite threat into an existential one. Finally, if he answers yes to all these questions he must ask himself whether this convenient alignment of reason with the promptings of his reptilian brain is not itself suspicious. How many wars can actually pass a screening process so rigorous, 'extreme vetting' if you like? I suspect the answer is very few. In fact, I will go a little farther, I will say that given the nature of modern weaponry and the multi-generational environmental damage they cause and given that a much more nuanced understanding of the psychological and spiritual costs of war exists now than a hundred years ago I think we can just about confine the notion of just war to apocalyptic scenarios of a science fiction kind. As an ordinary tool of politics I believe it is mostly bankrupt.[108]

But why do I say 'just about'? Is there a lingering doubt in my mind? I have to admit there is. I do not think the Norwegians who resisted Nazi invasion were murderers as pure pacifism would seem to imply. The defense of Finland against Stalinist aggression does not seem to me the same kind of wrong as the aggression it repelled. I suppose the reason is that our rights

---

[107]What is more all opposition and critique is assimilated to the capital E enemy. Critics of the war on terror are all sympathizers with terrorism. All critics of the left are Fascists. Once we have identified the outgroup as the existential threat we turn discipline and violence on the in-group, on those who seem insufficiently committed to or energized by our absolutist rhetoric. What is more fifth columns abound: perfectly innocent people are rounded up on suspicion of sympathy for the enemy as with Japanese and Italian Canadians in world War II. These are well trodden paths into which virtually all who venture warfare fall at some point. Scapegoating the innocent is one of the basic psychological mechanisms that take over when war is declared however 'moral' the combatants think themselves to be going in.

[108]A consideration I have not explored here but which is crucial nonetheless is the role of language in justifying violence. P.J Harvey has written a superb song entitled "The Words that Maketh Murder" . Words we associate with war (and have long associated with war, hence the conscious archaism of the title) are often not easy to parse. Security, for instance, often seems to be imagined security rather actual security. Terrorism is a subject of apprehension for Canadians though they are at far greater risk from raccoons. Nor are incidents of violence like domestic abuse considered a 'security' matter though they effect vastly more people and are far more deadly. Everyday 'accepted' violence is glossed over while more speculative threats are elevated to existential crises. Further what is this mysterious state of longed for 'security' which is worth untold real dangers and thousands or even millions of actual corpses? I could multiply examples but this one will do for the present.

are at the whim of others unless backed by some kind of ultimate sanction. We all recognize that without the implicit threat of force constituted by the police I cannot enforce any rights claim against others.[109] My rights in such a circumstance are simply theoretical. For so long as the concept of national sovereignty exists it seems inescapable that it too must be backed up by some sort of sanction.[110] If this sanction is an army or militia all the dangers and evils pointed to above will remain a possibility. That crack Finnish army that bloodied the Soviets in the Winter War could always in principle be used for less savory purposes: having armies we tend to find reasons to use them. I will say however that as techniques of non-violent resistance become more sophisticated, as transnational institutions become (hopefully) more robust, as people become more sensitized to the harms and indeed the corrupting influence of organized violence and its attendant structures... alas I find I cannot quite finish this sentence honestly. Is the human heart really capable of such a radical step? Can comprehensive peace not war be the default option? With a commitment peace comes, it would seem, the ultimate vulnerability, apparent exposure to the violence of the other. Any human being can take this stance for themselves but can we demand or even expect it of others? As Blake says in his *Songs of Experience* our hearts are armed with ten thousand spears. One problem with strict pacifism is the ease with which the *reductio ad absurdum* can (seemingly) be employed against it. We can all imagine horrific genocidal scenarios to which non-violence would seem a ludicrous response. Indeed,

---

[109]We all have a right not to be poisoned by our food for instance. If an inspector tells the butcher not to sell tainted meat this is not simply a request the butcher is free to ignore. This is because some sanction backs it up. Of course this sanction need not be lethal. Nor by police need we always mean sworn in officers of the law. Consumer boycotts are a form of policing for instance. Indeed, pacifists often offer as alternatives various forms of non-lethal sanction such as strikes, embargoes and so on. Still, each of these tactics has behind it at least some implied threat that the subject is expected to fear. Can one, say, boycott the state of Israel without implying that something bad will happen to Israelis? Or apply sanctions without implying that something will happen to those who ignore them? (i.e. that they will be arrested or have their reputations destroyed on Facebook).

[110]We can of course deprecate the whole notion of national sovereignty as such as anarchists and others do. I have two things to say to this. Firstly, violence is not unique to the nation state. It occurs under other social configurations such as clans, parties, city states, multi-national empires and so on. It is therefore hard to see why dismantling it will, without further ado, lead to a more peaceful world. Secondly, when I speak of sovereign states I do not mean the ones that are legitimate in theory (which would those be?) but the ones that currently fill the potholes and inspect the schools for mold. In other words, the ones that are sovereign in fact. If sovereignty were based on the presumed absence of moral taint then it is doubtful whether sovereign bodies of ANY kind would exist. Any society at all can be denounced as corrupt and illegitimate by anyone who cares to look into the violence and chicanery implicit in all foundings. Original sin applies here as elsewhere. Still, sovereignty is an effective fact we all recognize and consent to on a daily basis every time we stop at a red light or put our trust in the food we buy. People of any ideological stripe can look at the disaster in Iraq to see what happens when we declare sovereign states (even very imperfect ones) 'illegitimate' and arrogate to ourselves the right to dismantle them. In certain circumstances we may, of course, withdraw from the sovereignty of a state whose governance we find derelict or oppressive but when this is justified is a question for another time.

we don't entirely have to imagine: given what Hitler had planned for post conquest Russia it is hard to conceive of the Russian people doing differently from what they did, resist with all means at their disposal. These scenarios no doubt hold far too much sway over our thinking. Yet they speak to our underlying anxiety that the world is, ultimately a dangerous, untrustworthy place and that for our own sense of security we must keep the possibility of violence in our back pocket (this of course entails that it moves to our front pocket for if the Martians invade we can't get up an army out of nothing!).

More profoundly though many people hold the sentiment that the communities on which the good of all individuals ultimately rests, whether this be the city, the nation, the clan or what have you, represent an order of good that transcends the life of the empirical individual and must be defended as such even at the cost of individual lives (though *prima facie* this sits oddly with the notion of persons being ends in themselves). More importantly however I think this view lies at the heart of much *positive* patriotic sentiment. I suspect the Norwegians who inflicted such surprising (though alas temporary) reverses on the *Kriegsmarine* were motivated by the sentiment that the freedom of Norway was something to which they owed their lives and that those who came to take that freedom had (though this notion is obviously problematic) forfeited their own.[111] There may be no dispelling this sentiment among the general public if dispelling it were even a good thing. In such matters philosophers, like poets, can only warn us to be more critical. Above I have laid out certain criteria for doing so. Hard questions should be asked of *any* proposal to replace a state of peace (however shaky) with a state of war. These have been codified by tradition and supplemented by recent research and I only ask my readers to attend to them as closely and honestly as they can. Trudy Govier may well be correct when she claims "There is no need to go the route of absolute pacifism to criticize most arguments purporting to justify wars. Judicious skepticism will take us a long way in the same direction." (2005, 550).

---

[111]I once met a gentleman who was both a Luftwaffe ace and a staunch anti-Nazi. He was quite open about why he served a regime so repugnant to his political convictions: the allied bombing of German cities was intolerable to him on a personal level and he felt he had to do everything in his power to stop it. Such protective instincts are essential to human sociality and should not be lightly dismissed. Indeed, it is Aristotle's view that the soldier is the very paradigm of courage as he assumes the greatest risk, death, for the highest human end, the safety of the city. (N.E. III, 6, 25-35). Intellectually, it may be hard for us to grasp the ancient sense of the community as a supra-personal good but I don't think the notion is ever entirely far from human sentiment.

11 TOLERANCE

How much can a society tolerate and still function as a society? The question is not an idle one and I have no doubt that it has occurred to readers of this book. Astrology and Fairies and so on may be interesting from a purely theoretical standpoint, for instance, as a test cases for certain problems of epistemology. But should I be giving views of this kind an actual platform? Am I contributing to an atmosphere of 'superstition' that may have serious consequences as when people refuse to vaccinate their children? There is a corresponding question in the political/social realm. By arguing as I have with Islamophobes and racists have I not given them a legitimacy they do not deserve? Do I not grant a platform to people who create an atmosphere of hate and suspicion that can have deadly repercussions? Part of this problem is a legal/constitutional one which I will not be focusing on here. This is because I believe the crucial part of this discussion concerns not what is acceptable under this or that legal regime but the general practice of civil society i.e. those instances and problems that fall *outside* strict legal definition. I don't think even the most rabid of the proponents of scientific orthodoxy are suggesting we jail or banish Astrologers.[112] The argument is rather that we should shun them, ridicule them and deny them a voice. The same goes for people with noxious political views. Proponents of this view agree essentially with the old theologians that "error has no rights" . Not of course that they seek to revive the inquisitions: they argue rather that if everyone has a right to speak no one has a corresponding right to be heard. Censure, exclusion and ridicule are *social* not legal instruments for policing thought, for establishing the boundaries of what is legitimately thinkable and what is not. Indeed, they make the entirely sensible point that productive discussion cannot be open to any and every point of view (for where would such a discussion begin?) and in fact no society has *ever* permitted absolute freedom of opinion. Finally, the argument is made that a completely free society is a contradiction in terms: such a society would have to tolerate even the views of those who oppose tolerance and would

---

[112]This is an option resorted to by the Emperors of Rome and others throughout history. Among the Romans it was thought that horoscopes concerning the emperor had the potential to be politically subversive, particularly if they predicted an emperor's death or downfall. The medieval church did not care for astrologers either (at first) but by the 13th Century they were well established anyway.

suppress the speech of others. Genuine dialogue assumes certain ground rules about conduct and anyone incapable of respecting these is not part of the discussion.

All of this is of course true. Still, it does not quite answer the question mooted above, which is concerned, after all, not with whether a line sometimes needs to be drawn (it does) but what principles should govern the drawing of it. Specifically, where ought our bias to lie? Should we be suspicious of the diversity of opinion and its attendant dangers? Should any opinion that seeks recognition conform to an exacting standard of intellectual and moral probity? Conversely should we encourage the broadest possible range of opinion consistent with public safety and subject proposals to *restrict* opinion to the most rigorous skepticism? Where does the burden of evidence lie? Do those who want to restrict expression have to justify doing so or those who seek to unfetter it? Of course, we have institutions like universities that in some sense claim to be doing both; encouraging diversity of viewpoint yet insisting that any viewpoint addressed to the community of scholars justify itself in terms of recognized intellectual standards. Everyone has a right to express an opinion yet no one has a right to be taken seriously by their colleagues. Is this a model of free speech and expression that can be transported to the general society? Or rather does it produce the kind of conformity that needs to open up to new and challenging perspectives from without? The following paper will argue that society has both moral and pragmatic reasons to allow the greatest possible diversity of opinion. However, it will also argue that there are Kantian grounds for fixing firm limits to what can legitimately be said.

There are of course several reasons why we should prefer the greatest practical diversity of opinion consistent with having an ordered society. They have been given by J.S Mill among others. Let me consider two of them, the first regarding truth and the second regarding the process of uncovering and maintaining truth. It is banal to say no one is omniscient though it is a banality many of us pay lip rather than knee service to. However, if we are serious about the notion that truth is the object of collective search, that knowledge is dialogic, then we cannot dismiss the possibility that people who seem to us very wrong may in fact be right. Moreover, since truth is rarely an either/or matter I cannot dismiss the possibility that someone who is very wrong overall might be right in *some* aspect it is important to consider. Thus, by shouting others down I am denying *myself* potential sources of information. I am cutting off my nose to spite my face. Moreover, I am denying others the same benefit. The second point to consider is the tremendous debt orthodoxy owes to heresy. If the truth wins too completely then that is a very dangerous thing for truth. Without the stimulus provided by opposition our knowledge will quickly settle into unthinking opinion. We will forget the grounds on which the great questions have been settled and when challenged will be stuck for a reply. The reason there are flat-earthers is simple: the theory of a spherical earth was so successful that people ceased to regard it as a problem. They ceased altogether to think about it. Any challenge to the notion was met with scorn and indifference. Thus, when clever and determined flat-earthers came along *no one knew how to answer them* except a small number of specialists. Orthodoxy was caught flat-footed, made to look lumbering and uncritical and the superseded position began once again to spread. Further, nobody makes an advance in knowledge without critics. Nor does anyone get to pick their critics. Of course the historical norm here is to say thank you very much and subject your critics to retroactive punishment for making you think harder. However, as Blake says without contraries there is no progression: without the *clash* of ideas there is no *evolution* of ideas and the truth fails to emerge. This is a truth anyone who reads the tragedies of Aeschylus can see brilliantly demonstrated.

This is what we might call the Utilitarian view of free speech. From this perspective it does not matter *what* people say so long as their speech contributes to the *agon* of a market place of ideas. This tradition has, consequently, a high tolerance for speech that is offensive or politically and socially subversive. It has a high tolerance for unusual theories or suppressed discourses. The epitome of this tradition is no doubt the epistemological anarchism of Paul Feyerabend who was perfectly willing to invite astrologers and creationists into his class-room to test and challenge the assumptions of his students! I must admit that much of the material in this book is predicated on a similar spirit of inclusivity. However, we do not just speak of the benefits of free speech. We speak also of a *right* to free speech. Some speak of this as simply confined to the right not to be arrested for what one says though this strikes me as a mere legalism. Surely the reason we don't arrest people for expressing their opinions is that it is demeaning to shut people down. Surely the reason it is demeaning to shut people down is that thereby we are treating them as non-persons: as people unworthy to be heard. There have, of course, been many societies that have shut down whole classes people down because of who they are. In a truly democratic society this would not happen: background, education, religion or skin color would not prevent anyone from registering a point of view or having their thoughts or concerns attended to by others. We might call this the deontological view. In most circumstances the utilitarian and deontological views coincide. In what follows I will lay out a theory grounded in the latter approach. A theory founded on respect for persons is, I will argue, of somewhat more limited scope. The right of free speech on this view is presumptive. One has a right to free speech on the grounds that you yourself respect the personhood of others: thus insulting or hateful speech that degrades others has no presumptive right to be heard though it may provoke a productive response or sharpen the thinking of anti-racists. This because the presumption of any deontological theory is strict reciprocity and symmetrical obligation. This is the view I will proceed to defend though the results will cut across some of the current divides on this issue: while I will reject certain kinds of speech I will accept others that on the surface seem equally problematic. I can't stress enough that this is deliberate on my part as a theory that conformed too closely with my prejudices or anyone else's would immediately invite the accusation of double standards and special pleading. A deontological theory must be strictly objective and not grounded in any way in personal preference.

On both accounts of tolerance (utilitarian and deontological) the argument *ad baculam* is ruled out of court. The default mode of all discourse is persuasion rather than force or intimidation. Here we immediately face a problem for there are two aspects of expression: emotive and discursive. People want to make arguments and offer evidence but they also want to boo, heckle and jeer. They want to rebut positions held by others but also hold placards and chant and drown people out. In other words, one of the mechanisms used by civil society is ostracism or expulsion from the circle of discourse. Personally, I do not think ostracism has a very good history. I tend to think we can function without it in most instances.[113] Nonetheless no one is obligated to pay attention to everything and anyone is free to simply ignore discourse that upsets or offends them. As a university instructor and researcher I ignore and toss aside a good many things that fail to impress me. At the same time, I tell students that those who have the superior arguments and evidence have no need to resort to abuse. However, the activities described above are recognized modes of expression under law and it is utopian to imagine a world run solely on reasoned discourse. Given this reality we will proceed under the assumption that along with critical discourse there are emotive expressions whose purpose is to express root and branch rejection of a certain point of view. To that extent, they are a mild, if tolerated, form of violence. So, the question now is not just to what extent ought we to ignore certain positions but the extent to which we should actively prevent their expression.

We do not need to discuss threats and direct incitation to violence here as those activities are already directly illegal and can be dealt with by the appropriate authorities (i.e. Law enforcement or, if necessary, mental health professionals). There is a very real sense in which such speech is not speech at all in the sense relevant here. A level below this in seriousness is the activity we call lobbying. Anybody whose express purpose is to stand before an audience and tell flagrant untruths because he is paid to do so has no claim to be listened to as he is not attempting to inform or enlighten.[114] This is not 'speech' either in the pertinent sense as such a

---

[113]Advocates of what I call the 'boo-hiss theory' face a dilemma that seems to me unsolvable. Their stated purpose is to deny a platform to certain views yet the same protest tactics that suppress unpleasant opinions draw lavish attention to them as well. Who exactly was Jordan Petersen (to cite a notorious example) before people began protesting him? I sometimes wonder if people underestimate the power of an eye roll coupled with a contemptuous shrug. At any rate one cannot accuse people who seek discussion and debate of platforming when one engages in the showiest and most public form of platforming oneself. The ne plus ultra of this 'Streisand effect' was surely, as Alan Borovoy points out, the elevation of obscure cranks Ernst Zundel and Jim Keegstra to the status of public spectacles whose ideas were being seriously debated in a court of law. (48)

[114]At least no moral claim. As Alan Borovoy points out, however, not all the needs of civil society can be served by reasoned discourse. (24) Some forms of pressure or non-rational persuasion need to be protected though I would hesitate to go as far Borovoy does in calling them 'speech' as they are in fact legalized forms of manipulation or threat.

person is not a stakeholder in the truth. Their purpose is not to address the other as an autonomous agent but as an object to manipulate in the service of some inclination. This applies to political hacks as much as corporate apologists. Thirdly, anyone who claims that part or all of the audience they are addressing are not rational and do not possess human dignity is not 'speaking' either. An argument is addressed in principle to all rational agents therefore it is incoherent to claim that the rational agents one is addressing as rational agents are not in fact persons (ie. racism cannot be universalized). Every argument is an invitation to convert to a point of view and that entails the *possibility* of such conversion on the part of all addressed. As no one can change their race (presumably) racist arguments have no inherent claim to respect. All of this means that speech is real speech if it is addressed to the reason of the other and is intended to alter his or her attitudes, ideas or behavior. Any speech that meets this test is, it seems to me, inherently worthy of respect (in the sense I shall outline below).

This of course is a generous standard. If an obnoxious temperance crusader wants to convince me to give up scotch I owe his speech respect because, unpleasant as it is, it addresses me as a rational agent who can change his behavior. Foolish as it seems to me it is still part of the human conversation. If someone tell me that as a white male I can understand nothing about the world this is not speech as I cannot alter those facts and if it were true it would be a performative contradiction to address me at all.[115] It would be tantamount to yelling complex instructions at a cat. Of course there are grey areas. If I am gay for instance my sexuality is in all likelihood the product a complex web of factors involving fundamental life choices, formative experiences and deep-seated predispositions some of which may even be genetic. Thus, a fundamentalist pastor who fulminates against homosexuality may *think* he is addressing my behavior while *I* think he is denying my fundamental identity. This is because we are looking at homosexuality from fundamentally different perspectives. This makes this kind of conflict particularly complex as both parties are contending about something whose very nature they disagree on. In such situations a complex etiquette may be called for but the bottom line is that both parties must recognize they are addressing an autonomous rational agent primarily and an 'identity' such as Christian or gay secondarily. There is no possibility of peace between different perspectives if those perspectives do not merge in a common rationality grounded in our nature as autonomous moral agents. Prior to anyone being a Christian, atheist or what have

---

Borovoy's favored example of this is a picket line. A consumer boycott might be another example. The problem is that if one has legalized threats one may have to legalize bribes as the U.S. has done in its campaign financing laws to disastrous effect.

[115] A student of mine once told me, quite guilelessly I might add, that only gay women of color are capable of perceiving the truth. I pointed out to her that since she was white this involved her in a version of the liar's paradox. In all charity though I think what she meant to say was that marginality can help one perceive truths others fail to see which conforms quite well with what Mill tells us. Of course Mill would apply this to ALL forms of marginality not just the marginality of certain oppressed groups.

you they are a rational agent and an object of intrinsic respect considered *universally*.[116] Thus, the borderline (if my theory is correct) is crossed here only if the pastor in question attributes, say, some kind of demonism to his interlocutor. His speech is speech to the extent that he is addressing the reason and conscience of the other and if I think he is profoundly misguided that could well be an occasion for *me* to convert *him*. However, as a good deal of fundamentalist preaching *does* in fact harp on demonic or satanic influence much of it is not in fact speech (it addresses the other not as person but as the avatar of something non-human and is thus self-contradictory).

One thesis I am defending here is the notion of an ethical society that transcends religion and ideology. In this view the Baptist pastor and the LGBQ activist have common and reciprocal obligations of respect.[117] They do not inhabit distinct moral universes. The form of respect I speak of here is always and everywhere to address each other as persons. It is an existential challenge to ask someone to re-evaluate something as deep-seated as their sexuality. It is also an existential challenge to ask someone to re-evaluate something as deep-seated as their religion. An existential challenge can only be issued to a person, something I have noted from my repeated failure to get my cats to rethink their basic values! It cannot be the case then that a free society excludes the making of such challenges.[118] Such challenges need not be well received or appreciated. Usually they will not be. However, as we will often wish to issue such challenges to people we are bound to accept them in return. That said if I say to a Jew that the evil acts of the Israeli government proceed from some evil ontological essence common to all Jews then I have not addressed *him* at all. I have not

---

[116]In a perfect world of liberal neutrality, we could all respect each other as persons while actively despising each other's life choices, religion, sexuality, and so on. I realize this is Utopian in one sense. It is very hard for me to despise Seventh Day Adventism and not despise the people who practice it. In other words, imaginative sympathy (seeing myself in the other) seems a necessary supplement to recognizing the formal rights of the other. Still I cannot argue that the difficulty or absence of such sympathy renders the other a means and not an end. In this negative limiting sense, the standpoint of Liberal neutrality holds. Practical principles of reason however need to be brought into some harmony with inclination. Though we cannot (for purely logical reasons) have a world in which each of us can embrace the life stances of all we can always work to expand the circle of our interests and the range of our sympathies.

[117]For instance, there are neutral spaces in any free society where people encounter each other not as opponents but as citizens bound to mutual respect. Commercial space is surely one of these. The Pastor and the activist are, for instance, bound to buy and sell with each other whatever their mutual dislike. In any space whatsoever they are bound to respect each other's physical person however much the pastor may want to punch the activist or the activist may want to throw tomatoes at the pastor. I am aware that people are now hot and bothered about beating right wing extremists but this is tantamount to claiming society is in a state of war. This, alas, raises the complex tangle of just war theory which I have attempted to address above.

[118]This seems obvious to me but I suspect the reason it is not obvious to others is one of the peculiar delusions of modernity: the notion of an end of history. What sustains the viciousness of the pastor and the activist is the conviction each has that they are winning: that the great battle of modernity and tradition is about to be settled in their favor, whether by divine intervention or the necessity of progress. It is only when people realize they can't subdue each other that they begin to recognize each other as persons, as in the wonderful story of Gilgamesh and Enkidu.

challenged him to any act of human reflection as my words imply he is not capable of any.[119] I have merely used words as a bludgeon and committed a form of the *ad baculum* fallacy. Thus the pastor is free to challenge the unbeliever, the atheist is free to challenge a Jew or a Sikh, the vegetarian is free to challenge the meat eater and so on. The anti-Semite however is not free to degrade the Jew nor the Pastor free to attribute Satanism to the Muslim. In a free society such challenges will occur.[120] They may be accepted or rudely rebuffed. They may be turned back on the challenger. However, they cannot be suppressed. Note that in taking this position I am being resolutely anti-utopian. There will never be a world in which everyone embraces everyone nor is such a world desirable: the radical particularity of individuals will always assert itself and we will always need institutions and mores to contain the resulting conflicts. Thus, our prime minister is correct when he says tolerance is not enough but incorrect when he says it must be followed by acceptance: tolerance must be followed not by 'acceptance' of questionable sincerity but by *ethical respect*.

I take it as strong point of my theory that it pleases no one. Everyone wants an account of free speech that includes everything they like and excludes everything they don't like. There is no such account. So, right wingers will just have to accept that on this account racist speech is not speech. Progressives will just have to accept that conservative Christian pastors are in fact speaking at least some of the time. However, let me soften the blow somewhat for both groups. Any account of free speech that is not vacuous assumes that at some point we will have to listen to ideas and arguments we would rather not hear. At this point we should all remember that *we* often want to say things that *other* people would rather not hear. The tolerance we wish others to extend to us must be extended by us to them. There is nothing more frustrating than trying to get people to see that the restrictions they seek on the speech of others will inevitably be applied to them. I call this the magic bullet theory of free

---

[119]Sartre points out the conundrum the anti-Semite is in. To condemn the Jews, he must attribute agency to them. Yet for him the Jew can only do evil. Thus he must attribute to Jews everywhere a paradoxical freedom to do only evil. (337) Moreover, unlike the doctrine of universal sin, he must attribute this propensity to something particular to Jews (such as their blood). They must be the chosen people of evil. I suspect this attitude is implicit in the mid-set of some current day activists. If a Gentile government kills ten people that is a human error and a human crime. However, if a Jewish government kills ten people under identical circumstances this is a matter of much greater consequence as the evil in question is demonic not human, ontological not accidental. For the anti-Semite a Jew cannot, as Sartre points out (337), ever commit an act equivalent to a gentile: his act will always be the act of a Jew, proceeding from the essence of the Jew. As such it can never be morally neutral no matter how apparently trivial or innocuous. Nor can the gentile who murders a thousand ever be as guilty as the Jew is in the simple act of breathing.

[120]There is, I suppose, an etiquette to such challenges. Jehovah's Witnesses who go about issuing existential challenges to random strangers thereby render themselves obnoxious to others. This example however always gives me pause. The fact that I find the Jehovah's Witness version of Christianity beyond noxious in its sectarian arrogance is the very reason I cannot be entrusted to respect their rights as persons. They must be protected from people like me.

speech: the notion that restrictions on *their* speech can be formulated with such laser like precision that they can never be applied to *our* speech. On my reading (if it is successful) the conditions on which any party or side steps outside the bounds of genuine speech are clear. The limit of civic discourse is breached when any party addresses another party as less than human: as an 'it' that it would be contradictory to address in the first place. No one is constrained by such a regime except to the degree that they are simultaneously protected by it. This, I believe, is as far as we should go in protecting 'honest speech' while protecting society against bigots, shills, frauds and other subversives. To speak in Kantian terms, all speech should be respected which is consistent with a kingdom of ends.[121]

Now by respect I do not mean attention: nobody is owed anyone else's time or attention if only because time and attention are finite resources. Nor does it mean agreement or even politeness: by respect I mean consent to a world where such opinions can be expressed (and having so consented I cannot then pick and choose). This consent is denied if I disrupt the other's speech in such a way that that speech cannot be uttered. However, somebody with the virtues of curiosity and attentiveness should certainly attend to as many viewpoints as possible especially those which have been marginalized and excluded unjustly. Now however I wish to address certain objections I anticipate from those who think I am too liberal and those who think I am not liberal enough. First, my account is in some tension with Mill's in that there is speech I do not think merits respect. Mill would say that one of the reasons I would not suppress racist speech is the miniscule chance it has of being correct. Truth is not the sole value however: we do not use medical research conducted by the Nazis because of the immoral situations under which it was conducted. To do otherwise would encourage others to conduct immoral research in the hopes of finding something useful and winning thereby a get out of jail free card. Similarly, there might well be useful tidbits contained in the rantings of racists but this would not justify permitting them to speak as their position violates one of the fundamental conditions of dialogue. That said a world without racist discourse of any kind would, for the reasons noted above, be extremely

---

[121]No doubt some people will be uncomfortable with the implication that the oppressed and their oppressors are subject to common moral standards. Can there be universal moral standards in a world where power is not shared equally? Frankly, and with all due respect, I have to say there can be. I have no problem with anyone striving to alter unjust and oppressively hierarchical social arrangements. Any such activity however has to conform to the demand that we respect persons as ends. Why? Because (and forgive me for resorting to consequentialist reasoning here) we know what happens when we don't. This is a question on which the data is all in. We know that people who are not bound by ethical respect even of their enemies will commit crimes and atrocities. Indeed, the notion that we can treat the enemy as an 'it' lies at the heart of every atrocity which has been committed in the name of revolution. It lies at the heart of every atrocity committed in the name of reaction too. In fact, it is the principle that justifies all atrocities. At any rate to see the point I am making it suffices for anyone to ask themselves why their activism does not include torture or assassination. Prior to any ideological stance are what Leszek Kolakowski calls 'elementary situations' in which, say, I feed the children of my enemies exactly as I would feed my own. Without this limiting principle, he argues, politics can breed only monsters. (1968; 219)

vulnerable to racists. Just because we are within our rights to shut down a certain discourse does not mean that we always should. The effectiveness of the 'boo-hiss' approach is inversely proportional to its frequency. Ideally, it should be something we keep in reserve to employ when discourse is too socially disruptive to be worthwhile and threatens to provoke civic unrest or other social ills. Keeping this in mind we can satisfy most of Mill's concerns while retaining certain limits on what can be said and not said.[122] A liberal society, for instance, should be liberal in allowing its own principles to be questioned. That is a bedrock principle. The racist however, generally raises no real question and his speech should be treated as a kind of noise.

Others will say that I am being far too liberal: I call this the Weimar argument. Tolerance is self-defeating because it platforms positions that are subversive and oppressive to others especially minorities. Tolerance, in other words, leads to Nazism. Personally I think this argument is highly overrated. If the world is veering in a Fascist direction at the moment it is precisely because so many people *lack* a voice. Our corporate media has allowed a small minority of individuals to monopolize discourse to an almost unprecedented degree. Media shape all discourse in the terms acceptable to their corporate masters so it is quite natural that people have migrated to the wild west of the internet (with all the dangers which attend this move). The world, then, is not dying from too much liberalism but too little. A radical commitment to free speech is a commitment to genuine democratization and the creation of institutions (like public broadcasting) that allow for a wide range of voices.

Finally, there is the unresolved question of public safety. By this I mean that speech that is not directly threatening can none the less contribute to a subtle atmosphere of intimidation which can be just as threatening. To this I respond that the state cannot prevent any and all evils without serious harm to human freedom. The law, for instance cannot deal, except in a limited way, with speculative or implicit threats as these could literally be anything or everything: the very fact that I can raise my arm is an implicit threat to everyone I know. I think the same limitation applies to civil society. We cannot protest every person who collects war memorabilia on the off chance they might be a Nazi. I might *suspect* a collector of Nazi memorabilia of being a sympathizer but on the basis of his odd collecting habits I cannot *accuse* him without further evidence. We are bound then to shut down (either through law or through civic intercourse) only those

---

[122]While we do not owe respect to racist speech we may, in a given circumstance, grant it toleration. Thus, if a public figure is given out by critics to be a racist members of the public may legitimately ask to hear the individual in question speak and make up their own minds. There is also a real public interest served by knowing what and how racists think. The same applies to lobbyists and politicians whose aim is persuasion rather than discovery. Not being stakeholders in the truth they are not true participants in free discourse and have no formal rights thereby. Still, there are many prudential reasons for hearing them out. Conversely, while there may be a formal right to issue existential challenges such as I have described it is not always prudent or appropriate to do so in any and all circumstances, particularly when one is dealing with a hot-button issue to which people are simply too close. This is a problem of rhetoric, the art of adjusting discourse to the audience one is addressing.

speech acts which *directly* call the humanity of others in question. As for those who are cagey in their speech they should be called out: we should challenge and provoke them to say openly what they only insinuate.

To conclude: there is discourse covered by laws (like hate speech legislation). We are not here concerned with such speech. For all the rest we should have the same presumption of tolerance we desire to be extended to ourselves. This presumption is defeasible in the case of discourse which is not discourse but concealed violence: discourse which addresses the community of all rational agents as if some were not rational agents. In principle we have the right to suppress such discourse but a 'zero tolerance' policy is probably unwise in this case (as it is in just about every other). The means of this suppression cannot, outside a state of war, include violence to persons or property but can include disruption by booing, chanting or other forms of protest.[123] Use of such tactics, however, should be rare as nothing wears faster than constant outrage and the objects of such protest generally benefit from it. Speech which it is *not* moral to suppress is speech addressed to a putative rational agent who can in principle change his or her mind or assume a new attitude. Such speech can be a profound challenge to a person's fundamental identity. It need not be met with attention, politeness or 'respect' in the more restricted sense but the general right to utter such speech should be recognized however annoying or offensive we may consider a particular example to be. This gives us a deontological account of the limits of speech while respecting the pragmatism of Mill's approach.

---

[123]I mention property here as some have argued that damage to 'mere' property is morally neutral. This is surely an untenable position. As the Catholic philosopher Antonio Rosmini put it property is a 'sphere around the person'. (see A. Mingardi "A Sphere Around the Person" https://papers.ssrn.com/sol3/papers.cfm?abstract_id=910946) The will and interests of individuals are naturally embedded in it so that the distinction between harm to property and harm to persons is in most instances an empty one. Most property is entwined with someone's livelihood or is someone's responsibility such that damaging it has a real effect on persons. It is surprisingly difficult, I find, to get people who advocate window smashing (for instance) to recognize that somebody NOT a privileged university student has to clean up the shattered glass. On this question perhaps they should consider Marx who opposed bourgeois private property precisely because it alienated human beings from objects in which they had embodied their creativity and wills: the abolition of a certain historically determined form of property would allow people ownership over the products of their labor for the first time. (see Dupre, 132 for a nice account of this)

12 THE WEIRDEST IDEA OF ALL

If Facebook is to believed I am a staunch proponent of a terrible idea: that enemies deserve the same moral respect as friends. I don't think this is especially complicated. If ethical respect applies to any rational subject it applies to all without condition. Human obligations are mutual and reciprocal such that no human being can be an object for any other human being. Societies that commit themselves to this principle commit themselves to abolishing a host of historical evils such as slavery, torture, the abuse of prisoners, capital punishment and so on. To cite an example close to home, the principle that persons are ends and not means has meant a profound shift away from paternalism in medicine towards a new emphasis on patient autonomy and the disappearance as an authorized practice of 'benevolent lying' to the sick. Of course speaking the way I do is to use the moral language first forged by Kant. However, as the name of Kant seems to be an impossible bugbear for many I will drop all reference to him (at least as much as I can!). At any rate his great moral principle (the second formulation of the categorical imperative) is accepted by many who would hardly consider themselves Kantians in every other respect. I will call it E or the ends principle. In Kant's own words it runs like this: "Now, I say, man, and, in general, every rational being exists as an end in himself and not merely as a means to be arbitrarily used by this or that will" . (1993; 52) It encapsulates the fundamental distinction between persons, objects of unconditional ethical respect, and things, such as chairs, to which we have no moral obligations. This means that no rational agent (ie person) can be reduced to the status of a thing or an object to be used or manipulated as when we maliciously deceive someone or deprive them of their liberty of action through violence.

Years of teaching E to students have taught me every captious objection to it so let me eliminate them right off the bat. By 'respect' Kant does not mean admiration: we are not obligated to admire anyone. Respect here means to regard persons as unconditional goods: for instance, we cannot attach a price to a human life because persons are not conditional goods who can be traded for money. Another way of saying this this is that the value of a person is inalienable and cannot be commodified or rendered an object of exchange as when I exploit a person to realize some cash value. Nor does the principle say we can never *treat* someone as a means (ie as an instrumental good) as to survive I must treat the baker as a source of bread. It says we can never *reduce* the baker to a means, as I would if I robbed him instead of paying for my bread. Moreover, saying that human persons are objects of ethical respect does not entail that only human persons are objects of respect. For Kant of course God is a person who is not a human person but we could easily add alien races to this list and there are perhaps good reasons to extend E to cover at least some of the higher mammals like whales and elephants. Further, E is not propounding to us some 'abstract' principle brought down from an ethereal plane and propounded to us by an oracle named Immanuel Kant. E is a principle implicit in all our practical reasoning insofar as that reasoning is moral as opposed to prudential: we use E exactly as we use *modus ponens* every time we take the bus and it matters not at all whether we are explicitly conscious of that fact or not.

Now some object to E on the grounds that there are no moral universals: frankly, I think E is the single most compelling instance of the falsity of that principle. However, there is an issue that needs clarification so I will say a few words on the subject. Aristotle tells us that most of our ethical decisions are context dependent as the 'mean' varies from situation to situation (NE,II,6.1106b). He is quite correct in this but some seem to draw the conclusion that ALL our ethical decisions fall into this category. Aristotle, again quite rightly, denies this saying that certain actions, like murder are 'intrinsically shameful' (NE,II, 6, 1107a.). I think most reasonable people would agree that there is no 'context' that justifies the sexual abuse of a child. Most reasonable people who do not belong to conservative parties pushing a 'security' agenda would agree that no 'context' justifies torture. At any rate, such 'situationalist' accounts can readily be dispatched. If ethics is 'situationist' all the way down, then there is simply no such thing as ethics. Barring such ethical principles as E or the principle of non-malfeasance or the principle of utility how can we even identify which 'situations' or 'contexts' present us with ethical challenges and which do not? There is nothing magical about a context: a context is merely a state of affairs. Say this state of affairs is a mess on a table. The minutest examination of the physical context of this mess will not reveal a single thing concerning my obligation to clean it up. The minutest examination of the social environment of my apartment may convey the *empirical fact* of purported ethical obligations (I may *record* my roommates saying I am a jerk) but not even this will convey to me the notion of an ethical principle to which I, in particular, ought to comply. In other words, no mere description, no matter how fine grained and sophisticated, can convey to me the notion that *I* ought to do x because it is the *right* thing to do. Context tells us literally nothing unless we have some standard to apply to that context. To use the common adage there is no deriving an ought from an is, a moral obligation from any finite assembly of facts. If we can judge concerning the mess and who should clean it up this is because we decide to look at the physical state of affairs through an ethical lens that we *import* into it. In this case we look at it in terms of distributive justice, the principle through which we determine a fair distribution of tasks. We might in fact particularize this principle to say that things like gender should not enter into determining the fair distribution of tasks in which case I would have no right to assume that my female roommate should clean up after me! Of course, to anticipate a final objection, different people may argue different things about what exactly the principle of distributive justice entails in this circumstance but all these arguments will be made in terms of the broader concept of the just and unjust, what is 'due' to who, without which we would be staring blankly at a set of perfectly mute facts. I recall a neuroscientist who once said that he could explain everything about the mind but consciousness and free will: the case is similar here, the empirical observer can report to us every single *fact* about the condition of the table but cannot give us the faintest inkling of what is *obligatory* about it without introducing some kind of universal principle however broadly conceived.

Having addressed these objections to E let me move on to the main issue I wish to address. Turned upside down, backwards and forwards a million times E will always say the same thing: that ethical respect attaches to persons regardless of whether they are our friends or our enemies and regardless of whether they are good people or bad. In other words, ethical respect for persons is unconditional, like our love for our children. Facebook, the land of swift and summary condemnation of everything and anybody, does not seem to care for this fact. In fact, people seem think that E, applied in this way, involves some deep moral blindness. Digging into the issue with my many articulate conversation partners I have discovered why, for some at least, love of enemies is a bothersome principle. As Polemarchus in the *Republic* might have said loving our enemies seems inconsistent with loving our friends. In other words, there are situations in life where justice to one person entails injustice to another. I think this is entirely wrong: one of the reasons we have criminal trials rather than mob violence is that in situations of conflict justice must be done to two parties not one. However, a powerful appeal can be made on another principle, that of solidarity, and this will require some careful discussion. Theologians used to speak about a 'preferential option for the poor'. Perhaps they still do but I have not engaged with theology in quite some time. At any rate what they mean by this that any theological (or other) hermeneutic must assume the standpoint of the poor, the suffering and the vulnerable. Of course the richest man in the world can suffer the pains of the damned from gout or arthritis but the suffering crucial here is that of economic injustice and poverty. I have never been entirely sure what this means but I suppose one thing it means is that the justice of any society is measured by how its weakest and most vulnerable members are treated and that if we willfully refuse to see the world through their eyes then we cannot call our moral complacency and smug privilege Christian. Thus, it would seem that the neutral stance we take by regarding the victim and the victimizer as both possessing the same moral personhood is inconsistent with taking the side of the poor in all things. As one of my interlocutors put it to me, there are the people who are oppressed and those who do the oppressing: the former are persons and the latter are 'garbage humans'.[124] We cannot be neutral in *any way* between oppressor and oppressed without being complicit in oppression. Of course this is inconsistent with Christian *agape* as anyone has ever conceived it which is perhaps why secular revolutionaries who ascribe to the Leninist principle that 'ethical' means what furthers the revolution and 'unethical' means what hinders it can claim more consistency.

This is however, a lunatic consistency.[125] No sane human being looking at the 20th Century dispassionately can prefer Lenin to Romero however clearer a thinker the former may have been. There are a number of angles from which we may examine this assertion which the purveyors of *Sassy Socialist Memes* will no doubt bristle at. The first thing to point out is that my Kantian hackles rise whenever people point to the importance of 'context' (such as 'revolutionary context') for ethical judgment. Such people are as often as not trying to exempt themselves or those they admire or approve of from ethical constraints that they nonetheless think still apply to everybody else (as every thief condemns robbery when he's the victim of it). This ignores the fact that everybody else, Capitalist pigs included, also lives in 'special circumstances' that justify the claim that common rules apply to others but not *them* (after all, how can you tax 'job creators' like everybody else!). On this principle ethics disappears altogether: everybody is a special exception to universal rules that apply to all in general but none in particular! I share the impatience of Pascal and Kant for this kind of casuistry that leaves ethics completely intact while licensing universal immorality. Anyway, one requires no greater wisdom than is contained in

---

[124]To be fair, I am not entirely sure what my interlocutor meant by this statement. If I call a person garbage in the heat of anger that is just an emotive outburst to be taken no more seriously than any other. In this context however it seems to me that 'garbage human' has been taken up as a reflective category not a visceral expression of anger. Now if I call someone 'trailer trash' or 'white trash' I am putting them down socially and simultaneously asserting my superior breeding or education. I am probably not exiling them from the circle of moral concern. However, when Hitler called the Slavic peoples 'subhuman trash' he meant this quite literally, he meant that their lives were utterly disposable like garbage. Where on this continuum am I to put 'garbage humans'? Well, I would say there certainly are people who are, to put it mildly, called to deep repentance. This however, implies that they are moral agents (and thus objects of respect) who can and ought to do better than they do. This does not seem entirely consistent with them being 'garbage' as 'garbage' humans presumably can do only 'garbage' things. At any rate the problem is clear: wherever this phrase is on the continuum of abuse (and I suppose it does not really matter here) the 'milder' occurrences of such phrases when constantly repeated prepare the way inexorably for the more extreme ones. We have the entire history of persecution in the 20th century to tell us this, as reasonable people recognize when it is other people's language at issue rather than their own.

[125]Latour points us to the Azande on this question. They believe that witches pass on their nature to their children. Yet they do not harass or kill the children of accused witches. This is a contradiction yet the Azande are far too sensible to extirpate whole clans of people for the sake of a logical principle. (186) It is a nightmare version of rationalism which demands that our actions be consistent with our ideas in every case (would the Azande be more 'rational' if they murdered children?). Polish philosopher Leszek Kolakowski, while still a Marxist, wrote a very fine essay called "In Praise of Inconsistency" in which he demonstrated the enormous social utility, indeed the fundamental humanity, of being unprincipled. (1968; 211, 220) This is an important critique for any epistemic puritan or political ideologue to absorb.

Aesop's fables or Grimm's fairy tales to see that every little exception we make on our own behalf makes the next exception easier and broader.

The *reductio ad absurdum* of this attitude is the collapse, evident so clearly in the United States, of ethics itself into partisan politics (Steve Bannon is only honest in describing himself as a disciple of Lenin) where justice is only what my political movement says it is and any deviation from this principle is denounced as treason. Thus we have the dismal spectacle of 'my side morality' where every insult and moral misstep of my party has its explanation and excuse while everything done and said by the other side is subject to the least charitable interpretation possible. This of course is the simple and inevitable result of reducing ethics to power politics whether left wing politics or right wing politics: the impartiality of ethical discourse is the first thing to go when society is redefined in purely agonistic terms. Is that a loss? Absolutely. Seductive in principle the notion that politics subsumes ethics (ie. that the 'end' justifies the 'means') is bankrupt in practice and there are mountains of corpses to attest to this fact (corpses created in the name of utterly failed causes!). Consider the major 20th Century exponent of this principle that ethics and expediency are one and the same: Vladimir Lenin. Nothing reveals the tawdry side of Lenin's mind than the murder of the children of the Czar and Czarina. Exactly as in a Shakespeare history the young prince is murdered (along with his sisters) not for what he is but for what he might become, thus settling all doubt that the glorious dawn of the revolution was anything but business as usual. The ethical world cannot be brought into being by a crime.[126] Please examine the history of the 20th Century to see who was right about this, the 'abstract' philosopher Kant or the supposedly 'practical' Lenin. A man who can murder a sick child can murder anyone as he who can murder a single human can in principle murder a billion. This shows that it is the philosophers and their careful determinations that have the concreteness of human experience in view not the abstract rage of revolutionaries.

However, I do NOT think solidarity for the vulnerable entails any of these consequences. Here I am going to say a hard thing, victims can be bad people as much as victimizers. Indeed, as Nietzsche understood the victim can be animated by a perverse will to power every bit as devious and destructive, indeed more so, than the oppressor's. A kind of 'slave morality' founded in resentment and bile can breed moral monstrosities in comparison to which the open honest 'badness' of the conquering aristocrat might almost seem refreshing. These are people constantly attacking and undermining the life force of others rather than undertaking the difficult work of enhancing their own. Like the Underground Man they prefer to be sick if it means they can drag the objects of their hatred down to their own level. They are constantly positioning themselves as 'victim number one' to manipulate the conscience of the other and subject it to passive

---

[126]I thus reject the notion that ethics is something we can put aside until the world is just and we are all free to be nice again. It takes a staggeringly naïve mind to believe that hearts habituated to 'necessary' cruelty and murder (or even to lesser vices) will suddenly become apostles of light when the revolution is over.

aggressive control. Of course Nietzsche finds the epitome of this vengeful spirit in Christianity. I don't. One reason I don't is that solidarity with the oppressed is solidarity with their weakness and vulnerability, solidarity with their specific demand for justice and *not* with the destructive psychological mechanisms by which they seek to compensate for this. Absolute and unreserved solidarity with the oppressed *does not* demand that we identify with anyone's will to revenge (whether verbal, moral or physical). It does not demand we adopt their hatred of the *oppressor* as opposed to the *oppression*. Charity (to use the old language) is a firm and persistent willing of the good of our neighbor and calls us to aid the oppressed *and* work for the conversion of the oppressor who is in his own way enslaved and diminished by the system of oppression he ostensibly benefits from (how many men are emotional cripples due to Patriarchy?). Indeed, people from oppressed backgrounds often see this more clearly than those who presume to speak on their behalf. They themselves see the necessity of overcoming hatred (real hatred, not performative Facebook rage) as the last step in liberation. Hatred, after all, puts us in the power of the other like little else. At any rate, the demand that we identify with the oppressed is grounded in respect for their personhood yet this demand cannot be objective (as opposed to a mere preference) unless grounded in the unconditional value of *all* persons: otherwise we have reverted to the archaic Greeks and the friend/enemy put forth by Polemarchus in the *Republic* and decisively critiqued by Socrates. (1961; 335 b-e)

At any rate none of this seems to me abstruse or difficult. However, I perceive the problem to be one that often afflicts morally earnest people (and note that as Blake teaches us morality without forgiveness is a form of violence). To a hammer everything is a nail and the tendency of ethically committed people is to assume that all differences are ethical. If my cocksure demand to bring about the ethical world in one fell swoop is met with resistance, I assume that this can *only* reflect some flaw in the other person's character.[127] Ethics then demands that I identify and call

---

[127]It has often been noted that the sectarian, of which the moralist ideologue is one species, reserves far more venom for his own side than for the enemy. As Kolakowski notes: "That special, pitiless hatred which almost every organization with a political ideology harbors for its heretics, dissidents, apostates, or renegades is a familiar phenomenon. It is a hundred times more violent than the revulsion felt for undisputed and recognized enemies." (97) He continues: "Unflagging vigilance over its own meticulous boundary lines is an essential characteristic of every social group that can be called a "sect" - constant control to assure precise and unambiguous criteria differentiating it from the entire outside world. These criteria are of various sorts... and the greater their number, pettiness and variety, the more advanced the ossification of the sect." (98) Of course sometimes the sect changes its doctrine precisely to elicit an oblation of the intellect from its members. A certain linguist named N.J. Marr was at one point considered the only theoretician in his field consistent with Marxism until virtually overnight he was declared by the Communist Party to be the linguist most opposed to Marxism. (173) The sectaries were simply left to marvel at this decision and revise their views accordingly, hoping no doubt they would be spared the further humiliation of having Dr. Marr promptly rehabilitated! This sectarian spirit did not die with communism as the following commentator attests: https://briarpatchmagazine.com/articles/view/a-note-on-call-out-culture.

out this failing in what looks like an act of moral heroism to me but a self-righteous display to the other. This is one of those basic failures of human communication that afflict even the sincerest and humblest of us. The fact is however that not every subject can occupy identical points on the continuum. Subjectivities are ineradicably individuated as well as being socially and geographically situated. This residue of particularity cannot be suppressed for all the pious wishing of idealists and activists of all stripes and the fact that utopias are so often contrived to suppress this stubborn particularity only shows what is wrong with devising utopias. We have to respect that fact that as the Underground Man points out one of us may choose to poke her tongue out at the crystal palace just to remind herself that she is free. Patience with the folly (and the freedom) of others is of course a difficult thing but Aristotle reminds us that none of the best things in life are easy and that is rarity is a good part of their value.

13   OUR WEIMAR MOMENT?

NOTE: The Essays "Our Weimar Moment" and "Conservatism: The End of an Idea" (Chapters 13 and 14) appeared previously in the Social Epistemology Review and Replay Collective.

I, like many worried about the rise of Fascism in America, thought Hilary Clinton would, by however modest a margin, buy us a few years to confront it more effectively. Now that I have been disabused of this hope it is time for sober reflection. Clinton has lost an election now she would otherwise have lost in four years. The populist wing of the Republican Party would simply have found a slicker, more intelligent candidate who is not a walking gaffe machine. 2020 was going to be theirs anyway. The extra time would have been nice but the reckoning has come now instead of later. So be it. A populist politics of racial and ethnic resentment has triumphed; xenophobic, anti-intellectual and contemptuous of institutions and the rule of law.[128] This politics either points towards or currently embodies a Fascist ideology depending on whether you are an optimist or a pessimist.[129] Here are some reflections I have prepared on this crisis and though academics generally hate to be proven wrong I sincerely hope (for once) that most of what I say is unduly pessimistic.

The west, it seems, is having its 'Weimar' moment: its feckless elites are incapable of resisting the rising tide of right wing authoritarianism. This is not an American problem; it is a global problem. This is so firstly because America's problems are *ipso facto* the world's problems. There is no place to hide from chaos in the U.S. unless one disengages from the global economy completely. Secondly, the forces that have propelled Trump to success in

---

[128]Whether or not individuals who voted for Trump did so for these motives or not they voted for a movement which embodies them. All extremist parties really need to succeed is a base and one other chunk of voters, fellow travelers, who simply want to 'throw the bums out'.

[129] By Fascist I here refer to a populist movement which sees its will as thwarted by constitutional and legal restraints and embodies that will in a demagogue who promises to overthrow them, usually as part and parcel of some myth of national redemption. I think this applies rather well to the Trump movement. Others may differ but I will not quibble over a word. Trump is a destructive figure whether he can be successfully categorized as a Fascist or not. Thus, how closely his Fascism maps onto other historical Fascisms may be left to specialists to determine. There are, however, grave dangers to the 'Hitler' analogy which will be noted below: for this reason, it is well to note that Trump's 'Fascism' is very much his own.

the United States are active in Europe as well and no doubt his victory will only encourage the forces of reaction there. If a renascent Fascism wins electoral success in both the US and Europe will Canada hold out long as the lone island of sanity? Our own Conservative party will no doubt learn its lessons from La Pen and Wilders if they or their ilk follow Trump to electoral success. Indeed, when in 8 to 10 years the Liberal Government has run its natural course there will be no stopping them. They will succeed in the way extremist parties always succeed: by waiting for a protest vote to sweep them into power. Fascism (proto or otherwise) will then come to Canada too.

It is hard to feel sorry for the Clintons, Blairs and Bushes who have made this possible. They and the neo-liberal doctrines they shilled for are now in the place that Orthodox Communism was in the 1980's. They have no credibility with the people they govern and cannot move them a millimeter towards the good. Who really wanted another Clinton in the Whitehouse? Who wanted more trade deals, more 'humanitarian' military interventions, more bailouts and bloated profits for the financial sector? Who wanted more 'restructuring' and 'rationalization'? More wage stagnation and the continued decline of the middle class? The main pillars of the New World Order, trade liberalization, privatization, and perpetual austerity summon as much enthusiasm now as the Soviet Union's last five- year plan. Of course these things were never meant to be political or subject to democratic control. That is why they were enshrined in international agreements and enforced by the IMF and World Bank. Politics, indeed history itself, was supposed to be over and done with as people like Fukayama assured us in the 90's. Clinton, a child of this era, would never have done anything 'political' in the sense of disturbing these global economic and security arrangements. She would have simply administered them (one suspects fairly competently) while trying to sell the results to an increasingly alienated public. However, anyone who thinks this kind of bland administrative talent benign should study the ugly history of the Clintons' dealings with Haiti and Honduras, those whose appointed station in the Global order is to provide cheap, immiserated labor in perpetuity. [130]

This system, of course, will not change under Trump, it will only become more chaotic. The neo-liberals at least offered *some* measure of order and predictability along with basic constitutional guarantees (unless of course you happen to be young, male and Muslim or a Black victim of police violence). Trump however faces a task even less manageable than Clinton. Capital under Trump will be more aggressive and unfettered than ever. Ordinary people will be poorer and unhealthier than ever. To keep the

---

[130]For starters see Edwige Danticat "Sweet Micky and the Sad DeJa Vu of Haiti's Presidential Elections" (New Yorker, Dec.3, 2015), Dana Frank "The Thugocracy Next Door" http://www.politico.com/magazine/story/2014/02). Matthew Pulver "Bill and Hillary's Hyper-Capitalist Disaster: how the Clintons can apologize for a Decade of Deadly Policies" (http://www.salon.com/2015/05/06) In fact the Clintons critics on this matter include the Clintons themselves: ""We Made a Devil's Bargain": Fmr. President Clinton Apologizes for Trade Policies that Destroyed Haitian Rice Farming" (https://www.democracynow.org/2010/4/1/).

latter engaged increasingly ugly racial rhetoric will be necessary. At the same time Trump will not have the gift of another Clinton in four years. He will have to keep certain aspects of the post war liberal consensus in place to please independents. The result will be a farrago of mismatched policies. There will be great pots of money for homeland security, police and the military. At the same time there will be 'fiscal responsibility' promised house Republicans. Abortion may be out but gay marriage will be in. Muslims and Hispanics will be subject to various forms of legal (or extra-legal) harassment but corporations who benefit from them will be given their open borders and cheap migrant workers. Infrastructure will be massively expanded but of course there will be tax cuts for all. A gifted politician might pull this off for a time but of course Trump is in the Whitehouse precisely because he is a political innocent.

As a result, Trump is unlikely to please the constituencies whose expectations he has raised. His ramshackle transition team of racists, millenarian weirdos, neo-con creeps and corporate hacks already embodies every aspect of this incoherent program. When the inevitable disappointment sets in will Trump's base decide that he has been co-opted by the system he was elected to shake up? Will they decide that they simply did not elect someone radical enough? If so, should we prepare for David Duke in 2020? As some context for understanding this however we might try to define the idea that runs through Trump's and other far right movements: this idea might be labeled 'particularism' which gets at the common core of the far right more than comparisons to Hitler, Franco, Mussolini or whoever (illuminating as these might sometimes be). This idea is based on the failure of two cosmopolitanisms: that of Neo-Liberalism and international Communism. In place of this it offers nationalism and ethno-identity politics as the third way. Of course, this is nothing new. The wars in the Balkans have already showed us ethnicity is a powerful force in contemporary politics. Far right movements have existed for decades in the United States and Europe even after the defeat of Germany. However, it is now clear that the same forces have moved from the periphery into the heartland. The United States, France, Germany, and Great Britain are the new Balkans in that fundamental questions of the nature of politics are now mooted there rather than in the hinterlands of Europe. So, where Neo-Liberalism saw universality embodied in a vision of as humans as consumers and Marxism saw universality embodied in a vision of humans as producers the new right emphasizes humans as embedded in relationships and identities that are fundamentally local or at most national. Thus, it rejects any effort to globalize trade and invokes the virtues of protectionism. As it opposes the free flow of capital so it opposes the free flow of people: refugees are now 'economic migrants' (read 'moochers') at best and terrorists at worst.[131] As in the old European right there are no 'rights of man' but rather rights of Englishmen, Frenchmen and Americans. Thus 'others' of various kinds

---

[131] Of course in the real world poverty and violence go hand in hand rendering the supposed distinction between 'economic migrants' and 'genuine refugees' pretty much meaningless.

can freely be tortured, denied habeas corpus and so on. At the extreme end this rejection of a universal moral language of rights becomes a narcissistic celebration of 'whiteness' or 'European identity'. At its most benign (if one can call it that) it expresses itself in a nostalgia for old national identities perceived to be under threat form 'globalism' and 'multiculturalism'.

On the face of it this all seems grossly unfair: if capital can migrate about the globe seeking the best deal why can't workers do the same? Moreover, much of the current refugee crisis can be laid at the feet of Western nations and their blundering 'humanitarian wars' which have created chaos and displaced multitudes. At any rate such people show no awareness that the reason people emigrate to the West is that our current global power arrangements ensure that the West is the site of economic privilege and that most people who aspire to a higher standard of living have to move to attain it. One might as well battle the tides as try to stop labor from going where money and opportunity reside: again we have accepted this proposition with respect to corporations so why not workers? I doubt the far right would be impressed by this plea however: after all, they seem to think neither labor nor capital should go anywhere. They would no doubt say globalism in any form must be dismantled and national identities along with national institutions must be reinforced. Many on the left share this vision at least where buttressing the nation state is concerned. At the same time though they still envisage a post-modern fluidity where identity is concerned oblivious to the fact that globalized economic and political institutions are the lynchpin of any such vision and that to restore the nation state is to restore the ethnic, cultural and perhaps even sexual identities that underwrite it. It is the resurgent right that shows more consistency here as at the core of their vision lie not the rights of persons but the rights of citizens understood, as in antiquity, in an exclusionary sense.[132]

Here we are then, with our political options reduced to three nostalgias. We can invoke the glory days of Reagan and Thatcher though the ecological and social externalities of neo-liberalism are not manageable. We can turn back to the ghastly regimes of international socialism and view them through a haze of false nostalgia. Finally, there are 'identity politics' and 'victim culture' invented by the left but now fully and freely appropriated by the right.[133] This movement (in its current form) would restore the nation state as an ethnic, cultural and economic monolith and at its extreme looks back to the fascist movements of the 20's and 30's. Are we

---

[132]Perhaps this is less than fair to the ancients: after all the rights of strangers and exiles were the province of Zeus Xenios and were hedged with the complex etiquette of the guest/host relationship (see Aeschylus, The Suppliants). Similar notions of sanctuary in the contemporary world are, alas, the object of contempt on the far right.

[133]If some implied moral privilege is attached to victimhood, then of course everyone will claim to be a victim. There is nothing at all to prevent Christian Fundamentalists or campus conservatives from casting themselves in this role once the narrative has been established. Further, even the perception of a double standard in these matters will only re-inforce their conviction. None of this is to say that there are no victims or that 'identity politics' has not improved overall civility in many crucial ways: anyone who remembers the eighties blushes at certain things that were routinely said. Everything, though, is subject to the law of unintended consequences.

really so out of ideas? Is there no viable future but only increasingly desperate revivals of a failed and discredited past? Resistance is heartening and it is largely to the political left that we must look for opposition to what is perhaps the most corrupt Oligarchy in the history of the planet. It would be equally heartening to think the left is ready to undertake this task. Alas I am not fully convinced it is. The only left leaning party in North America (outside the fringe parties) is the NDP and it is shackled to the centrism imposed by electoral politics. Nor can it seem to mobilize the urban and rural poor who are among its natural allies. There are more radical elements of the party but many of these are composed of current or former student leftists who are as much a hindrance as a help. Students go to university to find and forge identities and so it is natural that they will tend to form cliques (a tendency magnified ten-fold by social media). They will stake out stark positions and uncompromising attitudes, issue unconditional demands rather than working proposals, and use jargon culled from the social sciences to reinforce in-group identity. The point of a political *club* is to be small and confer a sense of status on those who belong. However, the point of a political *movement* is the exact opposite: its task is to be *large* and this is incompatible with cocksure dogmatism and a censorious tone that turns off potential allies. Growing a movement entails brokerage, forging alliances with people NOT our immediate allies to organize rallies, sit ins, mass strikes, defections and so on. This is not an activity for a self-righteous minority who, of course, want only to *distinguish* themselves from less enlightened folk. What works in graduate school does *not* necessarily work outside the academy.[134] This sectarian attitude reaches its peak among the proponents of 'black bloc' tactics: encouraging private militias and paramilitary violence is an idea so devastatingly misconceived that it is astonishing to still have to argue the point. It is also an idea beloved of the far right who use the exact same language to justify it. As the sole resistance to the current unsustainable regime the Left more than ever has to put its childhood things away and resist the romanticized and fake glamour of 'revolutionary' violence.[135]

---

[134]Current discussions surrounding 'white privilege' illustrate this point. When activists invoke this concept they think, naturally enough for university educated people, that they are conveying the denotation of the phrase: an unearned social advantage adhering to a particular race. As advertisers are aware, however, the general public hears connotation as much or more than denotation and 'privilege' alas connotes posh schools and delicate lace tea cozies. As these things are part of the experience of a tiny minority even of white people the phrase is dead on arrival. Rhetoric (in the ancient sense) needs to be attended to as much as social science.

[135]And here, to be frank, I must confront what I call 'performative' leftism: the notion that policing simple everyday speech acts somehow is the revolution, or at least an easy way to put one's commitment to it on constant public display. The North American left is obsessed with words, no doubt as befits a movement whose milieu is the university, but apart from some real (though modest) gains in civility what have we gained from this obsessive focus but a spate of brutal neologisms? Environmental devastation and income inequality are getting worse not better and splitting hairs over vocabulary will not alter that fact. It may be the case (though in fact I doubt it) that linguistic usage embodies in a straightforward way current oppressive social structures (as opposed to Anglo-Saxon ones!) but I see no evidence at all that altering the former will have any

I am not the person to solve these dilemmas however. I am a philosopher not an activist and my only job is to help clarify our thinking about the mess we find ourselves in. In that spirit I offer the following observations. They take the form of a reflection on Karl Marx whose writing seem to take on new life in the era in which we live. Marx has been gravely disserved by the elevation of his writings into a kind of holy writ. Though I have deep reservations about certain aspects of his thinking (which I will discuss below) it is surprising to me how accurate a diagnosis he offers of our current crisis. I will not comment here on the strange tension between brutal dialectical realism and hazy utopianism that is the ambiguous legacy of the Marxist tradition. Nor will I be reviving such difficult and contentious notions as the theory of surplus value or Marx's arcane analysis of Victorian economics.[136] If Marx is still relevant as a prophet for the 21st century it is not for these things but for his central insight that Capitalism as a system is unsustainable: of its very nature it absolutizes the profit motive and the relentless pursuit of profit at all costs must bring the system itself crashing down. It is clear to me, for instance, that untrammeled markets will destroy the social and ecological capital on which they rest and on this point at least Marxism seems to me correct. Only a system where the means of production are radically democratized is capable of wielding the instruments of modern technology in a way that is sustainable and broadly fair. Marx got many things tragically wrong but at the beginning of the 21st century we may wonder if he has gotten this one thing right. Not ten years ago this would have seemed a ridiculous question: the consensus surely was that the second half of the 2oth century had left Marx's thought far behind. However, is it true that current conditions (as so many have claimed) falsify not only the details of Marx's account but its spirit? The reason for saying so has hitherto been powerful: beginning with the post-depression era and continuing after the Second World War liberal democratic states have been governed by a consensus. Markets have been given freedom to operate

---

significant effect on the latter. I support any linguistic change that makes for more civil or respectful interchange (obviously we are well quit of words like 'retard' or 'faggot') but focusing on this should never be confused with manning the barricades and becomes contemptible as a self-righteous display.

[136] Of course fundamental challenges exist to Marixist economics and the anthropology underlying it. Of particular note here is Jean Baudrilliard, whose Mirror of Production castigates Marx for failing to question the principles of 'political economy' as defined in the 18th Century and making a fetish of Bourgeois notions of 'labor' under the all- encompassing sign of 'production'. (28-29) Thus, Marxism, far from being a radical critique of Capitalism simply reproduces its underlying logic. I cannot weigh in on this critique here but simply note its importance. I will say, however, that confronting Marxist notions of labor and productivity with, say, the ontologies of indigenous peoples shows just how dependent they are on the theoretical foundations of bourgeois Liberalism. Indeed, the Lockean stance towards nature, expropriation as property through productive labor, does not disappear from Marx but is simply socialized. The capitalist expropriation of the surplus value of labor disappears to make the social expropriation of land, "waste lands" as the Manifesto puts it, proceed apace. (54) Progressive advocates for the rights of indigenous peoples will have to rethink fundamental aspects of the Socialist tradition if they are serious about accommodating the indigenous viewpoint on land and ecological responsibility.

on the assumption that in certain key areas Government will intervene to even out the cruelties and inequities of the market place, for example with labor laws, social security systems etc. The true answer to Marx has always been that democratic states have the power and will to balance the demands of the market with basic social goods to a degree sufficient to prevent revolution.[137]

Of course, corporations and their apologists have never really accepted this consensus and, as the post war interventionist state has been fundamentally secular in outlook neither have the people we now call social conservatives. If Marx is right the post war consensus that has hitherto governed us is inherently unstable: corporations who face the imperative of ever improving their bottom line can, indeed must, do so by incrementally chipping away at every aspect of the state that embodies a higher good than the pursuit of individual profit. Since the whole *raison d'etre* of the liberal state has been to make the world safe for capitalism and the indefinite growth it promises the political class must more and more cede to these demands. However, man does not live by bread alone: to ensure electoral success corporate interests must align themselves with nationalists, racists, religious zealots and other disaffected groups as these are the one great mass of people outside the corporate sector who regard the post-war state as inherently corrupt. Thus, one sees the strange alliance between evangelical Protestants, conservative Catholics and the kleptocrats of the corporate elite: both fundamentally hate the progressive state and wish it dismantled, if for diametrically opposed reasons.

Anyone who reads the *Communist Manifesto* will see that Marx understood this dialectic perfectly well: the liberal state will always be threatened by an alliance of Capital with ethnic, national and religious exclusivism, in a word, fascism. As the liberal state is, in its essence, aligned with capital anyway it will inevitably lose this fight, making concession after concession until it is fundamentally toothless and an object of general contempt. Ironically, given Marx's notion that the state must ultimately wither away, the Liberal state will weaken itself to a point where it simply becomes expendable. The resultant unfettered pursuit of profit will produce such environmental devastation, such immiseration of what was once the middle class and such a cheapening of core values in spheres such as education and health-care that it will not be sustainable: the question of an alternative economic model will then present itself whether we wish it or not.[138] It is

---

[137]Or complete ecological collapse. Whatever the consequences to the planet corporations have made it clear that they wish to exploit fossil fuels until they are gone: one can only conclude that they prefer death to the intolerable burden of ecological responsibility. So far no national government or coalition of national governments has been able to tell them no. Of course a government that cannot tell private interests no is no government at all. So far, the liberal state has been failing one of its most significant tests and to that extent playing in the general rhetoric that states are useless anyway and might as well be replaced by private corporations or anarchist communes.

[138]We do not suffer from a lack of such models but from an excess. Trying to pick one's way through the proposals of participatory economists, anarchists, mutualists, syndicalists, anarcho-feminists and so on is rather like trying to decide which of a hundred

not for philosophers to predict the future or to dictate to practical people what they need to do. I only make the general point that the question of *laissez faire* economics is one of the handful of human notions on which the data appears to be in.

Yet it is clear too that without markets (of some kind) there is no way to adjust production to the real needs and demands of individuals (markets, after all, long predate capitalism). The grim catastrophe that was international communism was both the triumph and downfall of the technocratic dream: a universal society devoted to the conquest of nature and of chance. I do not simply refer here to ecological disasters such as the destruction of the Aral Sea or nuclear testing in Kazakhstan. I refer to the entire notion of a state that absorbs society in order to subject it to authoritarian technocratic control. I think the lesson is clear that no party or political movement no matter how well intentioned can absorb the government. No government can absorb society in its economic, cultural or scientific aspects. This is illustrated, for instance, by the utter failure of centrally planned economies to meet the needs of actual human beings.[139] Contingency and difference, whether in the form of an economic market or a 'marketplace of ideas' or a culture of criticism and resistance *within* the state (in the form of a free press, political opposition and so on) are essential to a free society. As Robert Heilbroner points out a free market at very least provides a place where dissidents and non-conformists can earn a living. (1992;69) I prescind here from the question of whether Marx (who is still as I have noted a major social theorist) is to blame for the fate of Marxism in the 20th century: certainly Marx says some potentially disturbing things about a temporary 'dictatorship' of the proletariat where the workers, or more disturbingly, people who have appointed themselves as repre-

---

sects of Protestantism represents the true religion. I offer no opinion on whether social forms like these may play a role in a post capitalist order. For all this author knows they might have many useful things to contribute. They do seem, however, to embody one principle which is surely erroneous: that the community will never have to exercise sovereignty over the will of individuals. As will be pointed out below the most anarcho-syndicalist of communes will still have to function in some minimal sense as a state. I point this out because the utopian notion that the human being can, in her immediate natural will, embody the will of the community is a dangerous delusion which lays the groundwork for 20th century totalitarianism. One way of reading the current essay is as a critique of the utopian impulse as it afflicts both Capitalist and other societies. The problem with all these suggestions is that, for now at least, they are merely ideal and do not reflect forces immanent in the world, a thing Marx himself deprecated.

[139]Ironies abound here. Robert Heilbroner notes: "As citizens of the former Soviet Union are discovering to their consternation, a market system means the end of the long queues for bread that were a curse of life under a system of centralized command, but it also means the introduction of a queue which did not exist formerly- namely, standing in line at employment offices and looking for work." (73-74) The curse of a command system is the inability to provide goods in sufficient quantity as and when people actually need them. If bread runs low the command system cannot pivot and continues producing other items (like the notorious black lamps) for which there is no demand at all. The curse of Capitalism is its inability to supply a sufficient amount of meaningful and non-exploitive work for its citizens: one accepts 'structural unemployment' and alienated labor rather as the Soviet citizen made due without toothpaste.

sentatives of the workers, take on the power of the Hobbesian sovereign.[140] State absolutism seems set as the precondition for abolishing the state. It is no doubt possible to find a reading of Marx that insulates him from all that has subsequently been done in his name: such a procedure, though, runs the risk of turning his doctrine into a mere idealism, something that *should* have been a moving force in history but, alas, *wasn't* due to Lenin, Plekhanov, the backwardness of the Russian people or what have you. Does Marxism allow any judgment but that of history? Does it not seem to fail its own most fundamental test? I note however that many of the people who currently flaunt the symbols and language of international socialism are (barring the odd lunatic who still pines for forced collectivization) social democrats at heart or anarchists rather than orthodox Marxist/Leninists. Certainly their concerns over environmentalism and the rights of indigenous peoples belong more to the progressivism of this century than of the last.[141] Crucial notions for Marx are the technological conquest of scarcity

---

[140]Communist Manifesto pp.53-54. Of course, barring Cincinnatus of early Roman times, no 'dictatorship' has ever been temporary by choice. A realist like Marx ought surely to have known that power does not renounce itself. Of this section of the Manifesto Jacques Barzun comments: "Nowhere does Marx's imaginative weakness and inconsequence appear more clearly than in this mishmash of bloody revolution with reformism." (Darwin, Marx, Wagner, 188) This is harsh but not by much. Barzun deftly points up the naiveté underlying Marx's apparent worldliness: "One therefore wonders by what secret mechanism he expected that in this case (i.e. the violent overthrow of the bourgeoisie) men goaded to destruction and sadism would settle down into artisans of peace and order." (187) In any violent revolution you will have men with guns and men with guns do not readily give them up. Most likely they will then become a militant clique who appoint themselves as representatives of the proletariat assuming its dictatorial function. This clique will already be criminalized by a long standing habit of identifying ethics with political expediency. A revolutionary general (in a depressingly familiar pattern) then becomes the next autocrat after killing or jailing his rivals. A new autocracy is the result and as Eagleton points out: ". . . a Socialism which fails to inherit from the middle class a rich legacy of liberal freedoms and civic institutions will simply reinforce that autocracy." (43) Perhaps it is this dynamic of armed insurrections, rather than supposed 'material conditions' in Russia or elsewhere that vitiated 20th Century Communism. We might then judge the insurrectionist approach to be largely a failure. Indeed, the modern world's first revolutionary society still faces the problem of legitimacy (if the new order replaces the old why can't the new order be replaced in turn?) with second amendment lunatics arguing that the state rules only at the pleasure of a 'militia' (i.e. an armed mob).

[141]Assimilation of indigenous peoples (so called 'futureless societies') was as firm a part of Soviet doctrine as of Canadian or American Liberalism. Indeed, what could it possibly mean to be an indigenous person in the universal technocracy envisaged by Marx and his followers? A person who claimed and expressed indigeneity would be, from this perspective, clinging to outmoded forms of life (i.e. forms of life that do not reflect current modes of production) and would, for that reason, be counter-revolutionary (see German Ideology, 44 for Marx's dismissive account of indigenous societies). At any rate nothing could be further from the scientific character of Marxism than the mania for ad hominem attacks and personal invective typical of certain contemporary radicals. Whether a capitalist is a loving father or steps on puppies is perfectly irrelevant. Marx is concerned with how institutions affect the perceptions and attitudes of the people who inhabit them. Capitalism is not oppressive because individual capitalists are bad people. A capitalist system run by kindly old grandfathers would not be a whit less oppressive. To be fair though, this contradiction is in Marx himself who never reconciled the vituperative rhetoric of Marxism with its actual substance.

and the full automation of labor and this certainly now looks naive from an ecological viewpoint. It looks increasingly like a Faustian delusion to believe that nature sets no limits on the possibility of abundance and prosperity. To truly eliminate scarcity, we must redefine our wants and needs, boring as that sounds, rather than overwhelm demand with supply.

These considerations seem to argue for some type of social-democratic ideal perhaps along Scandinavian lines. This, of course, is not a sure bet. Capital of its very nature will seek to subvert and destroy mixed economies of the social democratic type because it cannot internalize the notion of limit. As such regimes cannot exist without capital they will always be forced to accede to its demands, particularly in a globalized context. Given this a rapprochement between Capital and xenophobic nationalism, Fascism in other words, seems like a strangely logical if, finally, contradictory choice.[142] For those who receive none of the benefits of globalism but bear most of its burdens it may well be a compelling choice. I should point out that in the context of declining public trust in institutions Fascist style myths of national redemption are fatally tempting. Of course neo-liberalism has laid the groundwork for this with its mania for privatizing public assets, often at low cost. These measures, along with 'austerity' budgets reduce the efficacy of institutions which can then be portrayed as inept and beyond reform by those who want to profit from their sale. In this the neo-liberals make strange bedfellows with many radicals who also call for the dismantling of state institutions like the police and military: essentially, both groups take as their target the modern state which one sees as oppressive of economic enterprise and the other sees as oppressive of racial, class and gender difference. Battered from all sides of the political spectrum it is little wonder the state is now an object of general suspicion and contempt. It is little wonder people seek solutions that are radical though radical need not always (or indeed ever) equal progressive.[143]

---

[142]In Nazi Germany this contradiction was only resolved by the personality cult of Adolf Hitler to whom, finally, the German nation and all the institutions it contained became expendable. The interests of Capital, the Army and so on were sacrificed to a war of national suicide of which the charisma and will of the fuehrer was the only binding principle. That this will was fundamentally nihilistic is shown by the fanatical orders of Hitler's last days, orders only subverted by the intervention of Albert Speer.

[143]The easy convergence of these two positions should give us pause. That extremists of the alt-right and anti- fascist radicals on the left closely resemble each other is something readily discerned by anyone not an alt-right extremist and anti-fascist radical leftist. I do not simply refer to their unbending dogmatism or their penchant for reflexive verbal aggression and ad hominem attacks. I refer to the deeper truth that both groups are fundamentally Gnostic/Manichean in outlook. They are the lone voices of reason and integrity in an utterly corrupt world where public institutions need to be smashed instead of reformed and armies and police replaced with private militias culled from the remnant of the saints. In other words, to use a theological vocabulary, their outlook is sectarian not catholic (political errors are often secular transcriptions of theological ones). Indeed, one is reminded of Hegel's claim that 'absolute freedom' finds its logical fulfilment in murderous acts of political terror: "Universal freedom can thus produce neither a positive achievement nor a deed, there is left for it only negative action; it is merely the rage and fury of destruction." (The Phenomenology of Mind, 604).

Here, however, let me address something I think is a crucial error. We are hearing more and more of the 'weakness of liberalism' with the disturbing implication that we need something *less* rather than *more* liberal to deal with our current crisis. This argument, as it always has, runs like this. Liberalism is committed to the notion of pure tolerance and is thus incapable of opposing the rising tide of extremism. A commitment to pure liberalism will thus destroy liberalism altogether as extremists will use the cover of bourgeois civil rights to subvert the state. This is backed, again as always, with the argument *ad Hitleram*. Exactly as the Weimar Republic was 'too free' so we are 'too free'. If only, the argument goes, the Weimar state had been less tolerant and liberal force could have been used to stop the spread of Nazi ideology.[144] Thus, we too, if we are too 'liberal', will meet the same fate. This argument is surely balderdash. Firstly, what was it that rendered Nazi ideology a fringe phenomenon for the second half of the 20th century? Why was it that for so many decades, fascism was the preserve of isolated cranks, street thugs and lunatics? Clearly because the post war liberal consensus I have referred to above had widespread support. When did Fascism re-emerge as an option? Precisely when pro-market ideology succeeded in destroying that consensus. It is simply wrong that Fascism has re-emerged because of excessive liberalism: Fascism re-emerged when liberalism was subverted, when liberals themselves sold out their principles to the emerging class of financiers, speculators and media barons. What is more, this is yet another argument curiously appropriated from the far right: it has been the insistent claim of right wing Islamophobes that 'Liberalism' is unsustainable because it entails the tolerance of "Islamists" and those feckless voices on the 'left' who undermine the West's will to fight with their constant critiques of colonial oppression and craven apologies for acts of terror.

Indeed, I find it odd that a rhetorical ploy used so often on the right has now been picked up by the left apparently without anyone noticing. How many times have we been told by Bushes, Blairs and others that opposition to some foreign intervention was 'appeasement' because some foreign leader

---

[144]The 'liberal' character of the Weimar Republic should not be exaggerated, at least in this respect. As the Munich putsch illustrates attempts were made to suppress Nazism both by direct force and the banning of Nazi publications. These ultimately failed because a divided judiciary and army (many of whom were sympathetic to nationalism) were unable or unwilling to back up the fledgling Republic. (see Spielvogel, 36-39) As Alan Borovoy notes: "Remarkably, pre-Hitler Germany had laws very much like the Canadian anti-hate law. Moreover, these laws were enforced with some vigor... as subsequent history so painfully testifies, this type of legislation proved ineffectual on the one occasion when there was a real argument. Indeed, there is some indication that the Nazis of pre-Hitler Germany shrewdly exploited their criminal trials in order to increase the size of their constituency. (50) The argument for employing street violence is even weaker: if it is morally right to assault right wing people in the street the law would have to recognize this and permit such beatings and assaults. This, however, would entail stripping an entire class of citizens of their basic civil rights which no constitutional democracy can do. We would essentially have private citizens declaring a state of emergency and suspending civil rights which is bad enough when governments do it (see the Maher Arar case) but insanity if left to the judgment of any random citizen.

was the next 'Hitler'? I certainly do think Trump represents a form of Fascism (as I explained above) but it is well to remember that Trump is NOT Hilter. For one thing his movement has nothing like the ideological coherence of the Nazi Party (as noted above) nor has he anything like the shrewdness or determination or even basic competence of its leader. He also leads a country that has a long tradition of anti-authoritarian politics and (for now at least) some functioning checks and balances. This is important for two reasons. Firstly, the Hitler comparison creates the perception of an emergency to which any response is in principle justified: what would one *not* do to stop the next holocaust? Secondly, this response closes off an important discussion. If the problem with Trump is that he is Hitler then it follows that his supporters are the new Nazis: this dehumanizes them and renders their concerns moot. Politically this is disastrous for many (though not all) Trump supporters are legitimately upset about the failures of the neo-Liberal order. Fascism does not flourish in a vacuum and Trumpism is not reducible to slow witted people deciding to be jerks. Identifying and allaying these underlying anxieties and tensions is the real work of anti-fascists though it involves less than exhilarating things like humility and listening to others.[145]

Getting this balance right is crucial for the stakes are high. I believe what is at stake is a crucial component of the modern project. I believe that there is more to the idea of globalism than the ghastly parody of the Washington consensus. I believe the ideal of a catholic and universal human society is a necessary moral challenge and a marvelous opportunity for human growth. Are we really better off retreating into the parochialism of pre-modern societies? Are we better off fearing and scapegoating the other? Are we better off with the old national rivalries and their attendant violence? I say this in full awareness that supra-national institutions in the past have taken oppressive and imperial forms (such as the Romans and Ottomans or the modern imperialisms of the Americans and British). If there is something to be saved from the ideologies that drove those societies, it is the idea of universality: not of a universal military or commercial hegemony as in the past but of a moral society of all humans. To use Kant's phrase there is a Kingdom of Ends that is unlimited in scope and illimitable in principle. We now know, due the simple fact of global communications,

---

[145]Exemplary in this respect is Arlie Russell Hochschild: "The Ecstatic Edge of Politics: Sociology and Donald Trump" (http://www.asanet.org/sites/default/files/attach/journals/nov16csfeature_0.pdf). Changing the narrative of Trump voters requires understanding the narrative of Trump voters. Russell Hochschild points out that this narrative is theological at base and very deeply embedded in the thought forms of American Protestantism (688). Appeals to reason will not affect it. Immiserated whites who abandon myth for reason will live in the exact same devastated communities as before and their view of them will only be that much bleaker. If Trump's base is to be cracked by a progressive political party, incentives will need to be offered to his supporters to trade their despairing 'deep story' for a more hopeful narrative. Clinton lost to Trump because she did not offer such an incentive in material, moral or indeed any other form. No doubt she could not make such an offer loudly and publicly without offending the corporate donor class, which is most likely why she did not even campaign in the rust belt states that cost her the election.

that the other is not a monster or if he is a monster, is no more a monster than we are capable of being. We have no need to engage in speculation like a Medieval person would have to concerning distant folk such as the Moors. Given modern technology the other is among us whether we will it or no. The universal society is a simple *fact* however much we try to deny the moral implications of it. It is a fact that confronts us every day in the form of the world wide web. To use the language of Marx the material conditions of society *already point* to the necessity of a universal community!

This is reflected even in demographics: no western society currently has any future that does not involve an infusion of workers and consumers from other societies. Moreover, the many people in the west who *do* benefit from our current economic system will not easily forego new opportunities for consumption: having tried sushi they will not go back to meat and potatoes grown locally. Lest both my right and left leaning colleagues sniff at the superficiality of the dining classes with their pumpkin lattes and craft beers let me say that there are many who enjoy the liberty of *cultural* contacts with other parts of the globe who will not give this up either. In other words, every western society contains a *cosmopolitan impulse* which will have at least some say in any proposed future and these people wish no return to the pristine purity of square dancing and tractor pulls. I do not mean to be flippant here: in small ways as well as in large we are coming to the understanding of Terence that nothing human is alien. This is the ideal that was once embodied in the old notion of *Romanitas* and persists though the imperial days of Rome are long gone. It is well to remember that the first wave of political innovation in the West was the revived imperium of Charlemagne, a distant ancestor of our current European Union. Western culture at its best (as opposed to its worst) has *never* been about elevating the parochial for its own sake. Almost from the beginning (in spite of its wonderful and lively vernacular literatures) it employed the *lingua franca* of Latin as the universal norm of cultural discourse. This idea of universalism always has and always will meet resistance for openness entails risk and universalist ideals noble in conception have often disgraced themselves in practice. The temptation to turn our backs on this tradition are thus ever present. Yet those on the far right who trumpet 'European identity' while betraying everything good that Europe has ever accomplished not only deny the evident social facts of our world but its deepest moral potential as well.

Practically this means working to strengthen such international institutions as now exist and create new ones that can exercise some control over the flow of capital and enforce common labor and environmental standards. This means, and my right leaning readers will not like this, that I am indeed a globalist. As the ravages of unrestrained capitalism and environmental degradation are a global problem they call forth a global solution. Similarly, my anarchist readers will also be displeased for I do not envisage the dissolution of the nation state but rather international agreements that will strengthen it as there is little way to enforce common international standards that bypasses national sovereignty. What, for instance, if trade deals between nations were used to buttress labor and environmental standards rather than subvert them? What if corporations that roam the globe looking for the weakest regulations and most immiserated workers were simply shut out of their own markets by newly empowered national governments?[146] Both right and left envisage a world of spontaneously self-organizing social systems. The first group tell us that these are markets which if left to their own devices will slowly but surely solve all problems. The second group envisage workers organizing into guild like social collectives which can meet all basic needs on a purely local level. Both of these notions belong in the realm of utopian fiction. As Plato long ago pointed out classes emerge from any complex social order: antagonism and difference are grounded in the ineradicable particularity of human experience. The individual does not merge directly with the collective but must be disciplined by the mediating power of civic institutions to regard the freedom of the other as her own. In other words, evil will always emerge as individuals absolutize their differences and the state (in whatever form it takes) is required to contain and harness these conflicts for good.[147] This banal fact of human experience has long been enshrined in religious and mythic conceptions such as the fall from paradise. To put it bluntly, the communes envisaged by the anarchists and syndicalists (or any other form of social organization that assumes a direct harmony of interests between human beings) will last as long as it takes for the first love triangle to emerge: for the first individual to oppose absolutely his subjectivity to another (as in the story of Cain and Abel). On this point at least the existentialist tradition (think of Dostoevsky's underground man) has a much firmer grasp on reality than the Marxist as it recognizes the necessity of evil and conflict for the emergence of freedom.[148] We might do well here to heed the wise

---

[146]Is it inherently irrational to suggest that countries which try undercut other countries by slashing worker's rights and throwing out health and safety regulations should simply be excluded from trading blocs that agree to enforce common standards in these areas? Corporations, of course, can impose no discipline on themselves in such matters but might they become so worried about the prospects of global capitalism that, like addicts in a clinic, they agree to have their hands tied by the state?

[147] It is difficult to know why anyone would assume otherwise. The impression Marx leaves is that in a society without class conflict the individuality of each will fall into immediate harmony with the individuality of all which might, for all one knows, be true if it were not that class conflict is just one subset of conflict in general. People on the same side in the class war are quite capable of utter viciousness to each other as anyone can confirm by hanging around Socialists (or workers for that matter) for any length of time. I have spoken elsewhere of the grave loss to self-knowledge that comes from the occlusion of the theological tradition. This is a case in point: without the myth of the fall people have lost a powerful skeptical check on their motives and can, with fatal ease, identify their basest impulses with their highest and most noble aspirations. It is noteworthy that original sin is probably the least popular Christian doctrine though it is the only one capable of % 100 empirical confirmation.

[148] And here I must register my fundamental criticism of Marx (at least the utopian Marx) and the point on which he has failed to heed his teacher Hegel. Total freedom can only take the form of absolute tyranny. Thus it is not in fact an accident that Marx, who gives us a wonderful vision of the possibilities of human freedom (see Eagleton, 19-23), has given us also a formula for abject tyranny. Marx of course recognizes dialectical opposition as central to history. This is what the history of class struggle is all about. However, the notion that these tensions will directly resolve themselves once the capitalist

words of Blake: "Without contraries there is no progression. Attraction and repulsion, reason and energy, love and hate, are necessary to human existence." (*On the Marriage of Heaven and Hell*, 1978; 3, 10).

---

state is overthrown is both forlorn and dangerous. Forlorn because it cannot happen (differentiation will inevitably occur) and dangerous because once the 'individual' has been reconciled to the 'collective' any further assertion of personal will or individuality will simply be a falling off from the good and an object of immediate suppression. The final state can allow no real opposition or difference to emerge as the historical problem will be, supposedly, solved. This is Blake's warning about the 'religious' who seek to dissolve the tensions of history into a bland unity. (MHH 16, 10) This is also the price paid for historicizing a religious symbol (the millennium and the kingdom of God) and attempting to make of it a literal reality. Thus, the utopian strain in in Marx should at very least be an object of reserve and skepticism: it is no longer possible to separate the hope of Utopian thinking from the specter of mass murder.

14 CONSERVATISM: THE END OF AN IDEA

I recently noticed that conservatism as a political stance is definitively dead. Truth is it has been on life support for decades. This has not stopped all sorts of people from using the term both positively and negatively. All sorts of people proudly proclaim themselves to *be* conservatives while others angrily denounce people *as* conservatives. The death of conservatism means for starters means that neither group fully grasps of the term they are using. The word has become utterly detached from the thing. Another thing it means is that an individual may have conservative opinions but only in the sense that an individual may worship the goddess Artemis in her back yard or live like a 17th Century Puritan. It is a private eccentricity with no public institutional reality. The death of conservatism is then something like the death of God. There is no significance to taking any public stand as a conservative. This is for one basic reason. This reason is that the victory of ideology in contemporary politics is now total and that conservatism is not an ideology.[149] Our political discourse is now divided between three ideological stances: the progressive, the neo-liberal and ethno-nationalist stances. So called social conservatives used to exist but they have utterly disappeared into the third stance as is plain with the rise of Trump in the United States and the rise of similar populists elsewhere.[150] There are now no social conservatives of any note who are not also ethno-nationalists and

---

[149]A fundamental problem with conservatism is that as soon as it defines itself vis a vis its ideological rivals it itself becomes an ideological construct rather than an assumed form of life. At that point conservatism turns into reaction. This problem was noted as long ago as Aristophanes the Clouds. One ace in the hole of the radical tradition is that as soon as traditional norms are questioned and have to be self-consciously defended the conservative standpoint is lost. At that point conservatism becomes a position duking it out with the other positions scoring the odd victory here and suffering the odd reverse there.

[150]The fatal weakness of social conservatism as a political movement was that it never articulated a positive vision of society leaving this work first to neo-liberals and now to ethno-nationalists. Its politics was simply oppositional: devoted to blocking actions against abortion or homosexuality or other things deemed decadent, conflicts that were and are unwinnable. On this basis it forged its foolish alliance first with corporate kleptocracy and then with strident populism culminating in ludicrous defenses of Trumpism from previously reputable conservative publications like First Things. (e.g. Robert Reno https://www.firstthings.com/blogs/firstthoughts/2016/05/why-im-anti-anti-trump)

indeed primarily ethno-nationalists. This is absolutely evident from their obsession with a purported clash of civilizations between the West and Islam. By and large Muslims share the values of social conservatives when it comes to things like family, modesty, the centrality of religion and so on. Yet social conservatives despise and fear Muslims all the same making it plain that by family values they mean white Anglo-Saxon family values and by piety they mean white Anglo-Saxon piety. That is the core of the ethno-nationalist position: that western Christian values are cherished not for their supposed universality but as the foundation of a tribal identity. From time to time the neo-Liberal stance is classified as 'conservative' though for no reason I can fathom: as Marx pointed out predatory capitalism rips the veil form all traditional pieties by reducing everything to a cash value. The proposition that limitless accumulation is the aim of life and indeed the primary duty of a citizen is consistent with no ancient wisdom I know of religious or otherwise. Conservatism then is no more. Is this a good thing or a bad thing? It is hardly my place to say: conservatism itself advises us that like all human constructions it is finite and imperfect. However, at this point the reader may well be waiting, impatiently, for a definition of conservatism. What is it that I say has died? I will proceed to offer if not a definition then an account of what conservatism is in the root sense of the word: an attitude to the world which seeks to conserve or protect those principles, values or institutions on which genuine human flourishing has always and will always rest. It will then be evident that people who use the term most loudly haven't the faintest interest in conservatism or conservative values and perhaps never have. Of course, I run the risk of baffling people (both boosters and knockers) who will not recognize *their* version of conservatism in anything I say. I ask such people to be patient till I finish my exposition.

I said above that conservatism is not an ideology: from writers labelled 'conservative' it would be difficult to cull a doctrinal statement. This means that it has no definition in the sense of a core statement of doctrine or set of prescriptive demands: it is, if like, the position which is not a position but rather an attitude and a practice. However, I can give you a living example of it from a much despised source. I find an excellent description of conservatism as a life stance expressed in the five pillars of the Islamic faith.[151] *Soi-disant* 'conservatives' who are shocked and angered by this should ask themselves why as these values seem to me core to any conservative stance towards the world. The first of these pillars is the *shahada* or profession of faith: There is no god but god and Mohammed is his prophet. Now conservatism does not inherently care about the latter part of this assertion: it is happy to recognize a multitude of other prophets who have taught in other parts of the world such as Siddartha, Jesus, or Confucius. The first however is essential: conservatism is theocratic in orientation. Humans are first and foremost unconditionally responsible to a divine order: to the standards

---

[151]For a rich introduction to Islam and indeed to other major faiths see The World's Religions by John Huston Smith.

which are ultimate because they are founded in the unchanging nature of God. No human being is to place any finite value, such as family, clan, party in the place of God. The regard the finite as infinite in value and as an absolute end is to commit the arch-error of *shirk*. On this basis conservatism attaches only a qualified value to the goods of this world: it does not absolutize the relative. No movement, no passion, no interest which is merely human or temporary can trump our duty to god and his sovereign will. Order is prior absolutely to freedom and in fact it is true freedom to recognize this. Of course this whole position is pointless if we do not know God's will. Fortunately, it is of the nature of god to reveal himself in scriptures, historical events, the exemplary deeds of prophets and saints and so on. God is present and active in the world. His will is manifest in the sacred teachings and philosophies (the *philosophia perennialis*) of the world as in the depths of our own conscience.[152] Indeed, his will is present even in those conscious non-believers who nonetheless enshrine the eternal verities (the good, the beautiful and the true) within their hearts.

For this reason, the second pillar enjoins us to prayer. Humans must remember and acknowledge both internally and externally the absoluteness of God. This is important because it cuts against the grain. Our tendency is to lose focus in the midst of the world's distractions. We wander away from our final end and our ultimate good. We put wealth, or lust, or power or anger at the center of our lives instead of the union with god we all intrinsically long for. We miss our happiness by seeking it in things that cannot, of their very metaphysical nature, supply it. This is why prayer, both personal and liturgical is central to a well lived life for in prayer we re-collect our ultimate aim, the peace that comes of divine union. This peace is the aim of all prayer even when expressed in its lowest manifestation which is petitionary prayer. Conservatism calls us to recollect those spiritual values that make for true fulfillment against everything faddish and temporary. It calls to put the eternal always before the merely modish and to this extent prayer is one of its liveliest manifestations as it a call to remember god in the midst of this world.

Yet our lives are in this world too. Conservatism rejects the pessimism of the millenarian and gnostic. It does not long for an immanent millennium to destroy the present world order but waits patiently for the fulfillment of

---

[152]This notion of a 'perennial philosophy' is central to writers we might place on the conservative spectrum from traditionalist writers like Rene Guenon to more eclectic figures like Aldous Huxley or Simone Weil who, while influential in some conservative circles, defy easy categorization. These metaphysically inclined thinkers contrast with the more pragmatic strain of conservatism stemming from the tradition of Burke and Swift. The American Russel Kirk may be taken as one of the last influential exponents of this view. One can add to this list the disciples of Leo Strauss (a far deeper thinker than Kirk) and Canadians like George Grant. What any of these figures would have thought of Donald J. Trump, a wealthy vulgarian straight from the pages of the Satyricon, one can only guess. Ironies abound here however: Guenon, a western convert to Islam, seems to have influenced the volcanic anti-Islamic rage of Steve Bannon. The paleo-conservatism of the genteel Russel Kirk also spawned the nativism of Pat Buchanan. Every stance has its shadow, the embodiment of its darker tendencies and ethno-nationalism seems to stand in this relation to conservatism.

things in the fullness of time. Thus, when faced with the worldly Gnosticism of the secular revolutionary or the religious despair of those who simply wish to be raptured into eternity as the world burns it counsels skepticism. Thus, as our status in the next world is determined by how we live in this one our duty to god is also our duty to community. Almsgiving is then a conservative value. Wealth exists to be shared. It is not an idol and not an end. It is a means to community and those who are blessed with it in turn bless others. Wealth selfishly hoarded is not wealth at all and thus *zakat* is enjoined on all believers. This is especially important as we tend to the selfish and misguided view that our wealth is the deserved result of our special virtue whereas in truth all good things come from god and god alone. As it comes from god it is given back to god as god is present in the neediness of our neighbors and the needs of our community. How vulgar then is the so called 'prosperity gospel' preached by certain Christians who claim to have Jesus in their hearts when they do not even have Mohammed! There are many displays of vulgar wealth in the Islamic world as in ours. People in the East *and* the West need constant reminding that the needs of the community outweigh the wants of the individual. This is part of our human fallibility, out tendency to forget our ultimate end for merely proximate ones. The principle of almsgiving is, however, particularly salutary for those of us living in the Christian west as our societies have made the endless accumulation of personal wealth their over-riding principle even at the expense of the very soil we live on and the air we breathe. I should note though entirely in line with conservatism *zakat* assumes that differences between people entail differences in wealth and that this will not be abolished but equalized through giving.

The fourth pillar counsels fasting on the sound conservative principle that we do not live for the gratification of the senses but for the fulfillment of the spirit. Fasting reminds us that the primary struggle in life is with ourselves and that the demands of the moral and communal life are at odds (often) with the gratification of the senses. Indeed, there is no substitute for the feeling of hunger as those who never feel it have no conception of the suffering of those who do. This is why great wealth so often goes with poverty of the spirit and why it is harder for a rich man to enter the kingdom of heaven than for a camel to pass through the eye of a needle. Yet fasting is only one letter away from feasting. As there is a time to curb the senses there is a time to release them particularly in the context of communal celebration. As Aristotle said long ago, proper self-control involves not just self-denial, knowing when to say no to our desires, but also knowing when to indulge them: one does not gorge at a funeral or fast at a wedding. Still, as giving free rein to our desires must be choice and not compulsion our moral training will tend to focus on self-denial so that our indulgence may be unconstrained by evil habit.

Finally, the fifth pillar enjoins on us pilgrimage to Mecca and why not as life itself is a pilgrimage? T. S. Eliot prays: "help us to care and not to care" and this is the core of the notion that we are pilgrims in this world. The world of time and space we inhabit is both affirmed and transcended.

We give ourselves over to finite ends yet leave the fruit of our action in the hands of providence. The finite passes over to the infinite as we give over our worldly projects and passions, releasing them into the eternal will of God. On practical level this is a powerful inoculation against despair as the world does not bear all the weight of our expectations (which of its creaturely nature it can never bear). Consider as an example the old expression "better dead than red" . Those who uttered this expression meant that the Western Bourgeois form of freedom was freedom absolute and that its potential loss justified the nuclear annihilation of the planet. Of course, Western Bourgeois freedom (though admirable in many ways) is a provincial form of freedom. It does not exhaust every possibility of human good. Only a whig-history-on-steroids view of western institutions as the inevitable and only culmination of human history could justify such nihilism. Conservatism will have no truck with this sentiment. History is an arena of struggle subject to advances and retreats. Yet possibilities for good remain in the darkest of times and the insanity of history can never destroy or even affect in the slightest the eternal essence of God source and ground of all good. In a godless universe, where this world is the only locus of good, history becomes a battleground in which the stakes are absolute and compromise unthinkable: hence the vicious ideological battles of those who think they have solved the riddle of history and claim to be bringing about the final human good.

Of course it can be objected that conservatism as I have described it here has no more been tried than Christianity or communism. Conservativism, one might say, has never really existed outside the elegant, wistful prose of conservatives. There is much truth to this charge yet it is, of course, true of all moral stances that their instantiations are very far indeed from their archetypal forms. Hence we get the characteristic vice of the conservative: the tendency to forget fundamental values for external privileges and the inability to identify what it is that ought, in fact, to be conserved. Still, on the plus side of the ledger, the conservative might well ask whether his or her own view is comprehensive of all its rivals. Conservatives share with progressives a concern for justice and equity especially for the poor and marginalized. Conservatives share with ethno-nationalism a concern for the particularities of language and culture over against the homogenizing tendencies of globalism and technocracy. Conservatives even share with neo-liberals a suspicion of totalitarian power, planning and control. However, conservatism, in the west at least, may well be dead for a more fundamental reason. This is because there is a powerful alternative to the conservative tradition and that is the *radical* tradition. All three of our contemporary ideologies have their roots in radicalism and are closer to each other than they can readily imagine given their current conflict. For the radical tradition the constraints imposed by tradition are in almost all cases artificial. What the conservative tradition would constrain the radical tradition would release. Radicalism envisages a flowering of human diversity, a host of new avenues in which self-hood can be explored beyond the stale platitudes of convention. This radical principle has routed conservatism (much of which expressed itself as cheap nostalgia anyway) and is the default position of most (if not all) North Americans.[153]

This spirit can express itself as radical egalitarianism or its opposite. For instance, among ethno-nationalists it is assumed that the will of the *demos* embodies the wisdom and good sense of the people. This wisdom would readily express itself were it not for the constraints imposed by various 'elites' whose abstract intellectualism has lost touch with the community and indeed with reality. These elites constantly invoke the authority of science, or education or expertise or data against what 'simple folk' can see with their own eyes. When the *demos* seeks to express its will this is declared 'unconstitutional' or 'against the rule of law' by lawyers or advocacy groups or other 'elite' institutions. The *demos* however, holds all such institutions in contempt and seeks to impose its will through a 'great leader' who is willing to flout them and indeed is willing to flout moral convention altogether (even moral conventions like marital fidelity to which the *demos* remain sentimentally attached). Thus, we have a kind of direct democracy outside of constitutional and legal constraints such as conservatism has forever warned against. That these radicals sometimes espouse 'conservative' seeming policies or points of view is irrelevant as they espouse them lawlessly and in a manner contemptuous of the very traditions they claim to value. Why, for instance, is it conservative to despise the opinions of the educated and even pour contempt on the intellect itself? Such things are an expression of a rebellious and anti-authoritarian spirit. The *demos* trusts only in its collective judgment and not only rejects but actively despises any other principle. That this attitude is over-determined by socio-economic factors is plain but that does not make it any easier to deal with on a day to day basis especially as the scapegoating of immigrants, prisoners and others is high on the populist wish-list and the populace resents institutional constraints on its will to revenge especially.[154]

There is of course the other side of this coin and that is the populism of progressive movements such as the occupy movement, black-bloc radicals and so on.[155] These movements, it must be said, have aims that

---

[153] Any defense of a conservative principle in politics and society in the west can only be a highly qualified one for the reason that there are (in my view at least) a plurality of moral languages with claims on our attention and one of these is indeed that of the radical tradition. For Westerners this problem is acute for, as far as I able to determine, the roots of radicalism are in the Gospels and the Epistles of Paul. These are not Conservative documents in my reading of them precisely for their doctrine of radical solidarity with the poor which undermines the binaries on which traditional human societies are built (and sometimes subverts those texts themselves). It was not for nothing that the Emperors of Rome thought Christianity a fundamental threat to civilized standards. In the West, then, the radical principle is already present in its primary theological constitution (however much it tries to ignore or forget that fact).

[154] Indeed, conservative Christianity is, with some honorable exceptions, becoming a pharisaical revenge cult. Behind all the rhetoric around 'security' (Canada remains one of the securest societies on planet Earth where terrorism is concerned) and the 'Muslim threat' one will find the simple will to retaliate in kind against anyone who represents the hated 'other' no matter how guilty or how innocent.

[155] I have before me the online Anarchist Library compiled by the Green Mountain Collective. (https://theanarchistlibrary.org/library/anti-racist-action-the-green-mountain-

seem overall nobler and better than the beefs and resentments of populists. However, this is a weakness as much as a strength: as I said above every stance struggles with its shadow. Noble ideals are a proven danger when not accompanied by political and moral pragmatism and relentless self-examination. Moral crusaders have a distressing tendency to fumble badly when actually called upon to run things: this is because sweeping moral denunciations are a form of cheap grace while actual governance (self-governance included) is slow, patient work. There is also a false innocence that can maintained simply by never facing the temptations of power. William Blake (a far deeper radical) was a persistent critic of any form of abstract moralism. For him no political or theological order could be the basis of freedom that did not overcome the problem of self-righteousness: our tendency to identify ourselves with an abstract principle of goodness and others (inevitably) with an abstract principle of evil. In a powerful image he tells us that blood sacrifice and war are the culmination of the moral law, the categories of good and evil unrelieved by charity, solidarity, or forgiveness.[156] Moralism is for Blake a form of violence. (*Jerusalem*, 1978;47-51) Our care must embrace the 'minute particulars' of humanity: no 'humanism' can be liberating that puts an abstraction like 'Humanity' before flesh and blood human beings. We all have encountered people who virtue signal on every conceivable 'issue' but have little but venom in their hearts: one danger of the progressive stance lies, then, in the monsters of self-righteous zeal that it breeds.

At any rate, such people envisage (after some difficult to specify revolutionary event) a world in which a host of sexualities, ethnicities, personalities and identities flourish without constraint and (though this is surely impossible) without mutual contradiction.[157] As the economic discipline of

anarchist-collective-black-bloc-tactics-communique). These sources give the inescapable impression of an abstract ideological rage consuming itself in an intellectual and historical vacuum: pretty much as Hegel saw the French revolutionaries. (The Phenomenology of Mind, 604) Talking to proponents of these views online (if talking is quite the word for it) only deepens this impression. Perhaps I am being harsh however: if the reader is curious, she may peruse Hegel's chapter 'Absolute Freedom and Terror' and judge for herself if the comparison is apt. Those curious as to why the revolution always eats itself and why revolutionaries must at last turn on themselves may find Hegel's analysis helpful.

[156]That 'progressives' will verbally disembowel each other over ideological differences barely discernible to outsiders shows that they are far from immune to the mimetic violence described by Rene Girard (2001; 24-31) Just as Blake said, moral abstraction enacts ritual violence. Progressivism is far from alone in this of course and indeed the ethno-nationalist stance is even more Manichean and violent. Still, the fact that it is over all the most humane of the current stances only makes the trap deeper: without what theologians once called a sense of sin it is difficult to imagine any politics escaping the scapegoating impulse and the self-righteous violence it manifests. Considering the ridicule and anger one provokes from many progressives by defending a stance of non-violence things do not seem hopeful.

[157]This is a deeper problem than many realize. The total liberation of one standpoint is the suppression of another: unconditional solidarity with ALL standpoints at once seems a chimerical notion. This is why in practice progressives (for instance) must always favor some oppressed people over others: aboriginal people in Guatemala, say, over outlandish folk like the Copts in Egypt. This why the radical stance may, for all protestations to

Capitalism lies behind all other forms of oppression the current economic order must be overthrown. The suggested alternative is often some form of anarchism. Like the populists, anarchists distrust and despise constitutionalism which after all only serves to protect the oppressors. Indeed, the anarchists despise traditional civil liberties as a form of constraint and mock those who espouse them as 'liberals'. In particular, they resent the fact that such liberties prevent them from waging all-out war against their eternal adversary the populists. The populists heartily agree. Both sides fantasize about epic street confrontations or cyber battles that will issue in a final rout of the forces of evil. In other words, they are secular (and indeed religious) millenarians. Each believes in a great battle, an apocalyptic convulsion that will only happen if liberals and other idiots get out of the way. A significant minority of each group considers this not just as a 'culture war' but as a 'war' war with brickbats, fires and vandalism of property. At any rate both agree on the Manichean position: the world and everything in it is hopelessly vitiated and corrupt and must be purged by fire whether this be the literal fire of Armageddon or the flames of secular revolution.

Finally, we have the technological dreamers. They do not dream of an unconstrained populist will or an unconstrained flowering of genders and sexualities but of the unconstrained power of technical and economic innovation. The enemy is, again the state and its institutions. Regulation of industry and common sense controls over heedless technological advancement are as bizarre and repellent to them as constraints on abortion or sexuality are to progressives. They, after all, represent the creative energy behind all forms of human advancement, all growth and prosperity. Technological or business imperatives cannot be questioned without questioning prosperity and progress themselves: the two things which for this ideology are non-negotiable. Such people see nothing ironic or odd in the fact the

---

the contrary, be implicitly totalitarian. Consider the following problem: A adopts the deep narrative about himself that he is the one true prophet of God. A desires not only the liberty to adopt this self-description but demands the universal recognition of this deep description by others. It is, to him, a fundamental denial of his personhood should anyone question his foundational narrative as, in his mind, he IS this narrative. However, trouble arises if B also adopts the deep story that SHE is the one true prophet of God as others cannot offer unconditional affirmation of both narratives. Here is where the currently much maligned standpoint of liberalism steps in. The liberal defers the eschaton by imposing articles of peace on A and B while each prosecutes their claim to be the one true prophet. With this peace imposed A and B come to the realization that, whatever differences divide them, they share a common nature as rational agents. They can now differ on each other's deep story, neither one need be forced to accept the other because neither party is reducible to their narrative. With that they can go about their affairs. The alternative is playing the zero sum game of establishing my narrative as the dominant one through the suppression of the other contrary narrative. A simply destroys B. This is the totalitarian stance. Its dangers are evident yet the liberal stance costs as well. By entering that stance, we forgo universal recognition for the sake of peace and subordinate our deep story to the common good, at which point we cease to be simply our story, we assume a common public narrative as our own somewhat as we give up our private religious perceptions to join a church. I tend to think that is a cost worth paying though others may differ.

demands of progress and the spread of prosperity never conflict with their own self-interest. The self- interest of the entrepreneur or innovator *is* the interest of the community. In a seeming parody of the Marxist utopia where the freedom of each is the freedom of all the neo-liberals and libertarians do not see the economic freedom of the individual as ever conflicting with the good of the community. This is, of course, the dream of anarchists as well: that individual wills can exist in immediate and natural harmony once the power of the state is gone. The technophiles go even further however: for them this harmony can be achieved and maintained in the midst of unrestrained *competition*. The magic of the market will smooth out all inequities and bring prosperity and balance to all (or, if the libertarian leans also to vengeful populism, to the *deserving*). At any rate the neo-liberals have one ace in the hole that it is difficult to imagine anyone overcoming: this is the fact that almost all acts of rebellion can be appropriated and monetized. This is particularly true of physical vandalism. Capitalism does not fetishize physical property the way some anarchists think it does: burn a bank to the ground and you will find only that stock in private security companies has gone up.

For all three groups the enemy is clear as is the goal: the repressed must be liberated. The demos must be free to enact its vengeful fantasies on immigrants, prisoners or gays. The libertarian must be free to innovate and make more money than anyone can find a use for. Sexual and ethnic minorities must be free to express their forms of life to whatever limit logic implies. All must be free and all must be free especially of the enemy of freedom, the state and its laws and institutions.[158] This is the core of each position quite apart from the fact that within each there may be many demands reasonable in themselves. This indicates that the radical stance is *the* stance where our politics is concerned. Everything must be liberated though conservatives may warn again and again that liberation may mean the freedom of everything awful as easily as the freedom of everything good. Lamentation however is pointless (with apologies to Canada's lamenter-in-chief George Parkin Grant!). This is because the radical principle is *our* principle and is, indeed, along with conservatism, a fundamental human option. Moreover, it has great achievements to its credit even as conservatism has many disgraces.

At the same time radicalism imposes its own constraints: most of us would rejoice if anti-vaxxers stopped being such fools yet they are acting on an impeccable radical principle, that of personal autonomy, as well as a

---

[158] This is why the most embattled principle of all is the centrism espoused by the Democratic party in the U.S. and the Liberal Party in Canada. As in the thirties it seems "the center cannot hold" (to quote W.B. Yeats). The basic problem seems to me that no centrist government can impose discipline on the fossil fuel-industry. Nor can it impose any discipline on the speculators and financiers who hoard badly needed funds offshore: a miserly activity contrary to the very nature of the capitalism they are said to espouse. That said, if there is anything which can be said to be 'conservative' in the current context it is belief in a social democratic state with traditional civil liberties protected by a strong constitutional framework. This, if I would hazard a guess, would be the best polity currently on offer.

suspicion of institutionalized medicine that many of us share. In fact, this example raises a vexing problem: vaccination can only be carried out on a population, all must buy into it for it to work. How would an anarchist society founded on a principle of radical freedom (whether anarcho-communist or right wing patriot) handle a question of this sort? Will radical stances license such appalling disorder that conservatism will become a living option? Are Clinton and Trudeau after all the best we can hope for? Blake certainly painted a dark vision of the hellish cycle of rebellion and reaction: the perpetual alteration between sanguinary radicalism and stultifying conservatism. Is this our future? Philosophy, alas, does not deal with the future. It counsels only that we temper hope as well as fear and judge all things *sub-specie-aeternitatis*. It is with this stoic sentiment, as boring as it is true, that I will conclude. We seem at an impasse though the author would certainly be happy to learn from others that he is unduly pessimistic about the world.

References

Abdel, Haleem, Mohammed. 1999. *Understanding the Qu'ran* I.B. Tauris Publishers, New York.

Aeschylus. 1961. "The Suppliants." In *Prometheus Bound and Other Plays*, translated by Philip Vellacott, page numbers. London: Penguin Classics.

Ahmad, Asam. 2015. "A Note on Call-Out Culture." Briarpatch, March 2, 2015. https://briarpatchmagazine.com/articles/view/a-note-on-call-out-culture

Akroyd, Peter. 1995. *Blake* Minerva, London.

Aquinas, Thomas. 1997. *Basic Writings of Saint Thomas Aquinas* Hackett Publishing, Indianapolis.

Aristotle. 1942. *Metaphysics* in *The Basic Works of Aristotle* trans. R. McKeon. Random House, New York.

——. *Nichomachean Ethics*

Augustine, 1958. *On Christian Doctrine* MacMillan Publishing Company, New York.

Barzun, Jacques. 1958. *Darwin, Marx, Wagner: Critique of a Heritage.* New York: Doubleday Books.

Baudrilliard, Jean. 1975. *The Mirror of Production* Trans. Mark Poster. Telos Press, St. Louis.

Blake, William. 1978. "The Marriage of Heaven and Hell." In *The Complete Poems*, edited by Alicia Ostriker, London: Penguin Classics.

——. *The Mental Traveler*

——. *Europe: A Prophecy*

—— *Jerusalem*

—— *Letter to Thomas Butts*

Bloom, Paul. "Scientific Faith is Different from Religious Faith" *Atlantic Monthly*, November 24.

Blum, George P. 1998. *The Rise of Fascism in Europe.* Westport: Greenwood Press.

Boethius, 1969. *The Consolation of Philosophy* Penguin Classics, London.

Borovoy, Alan. *When Freedoms Collide* Lester & Orpin Dennys, Toronto, 1988.

Bracken, Henry. 1981. "Essence, Accident and Race." in L. Stevenson, *The Study of Human Nature* Oxford University Press, Oxford. 258-269

Brunk, Conrad. 2005 "Is Pacifism Morally Coherent" in *Contemporary Moral Issues* McGrath Hill Ryerson, Toronto. 513-525

Burton, Robert. 1972. *The Anatomy of Melancholy* J.M. Dent & Sons Ltd., London

The Catholic Study Bible 1990. Oxford University Press, Oxford.

—— *Epistle to the Galatians*

—- *The Gospel of John*

—— *The Gospel of Matthew*

—— *Isaiah*

Cobern, William W., and Cathleen C. Loving. 2000. "Defining 'science' in a multicultural world: Implications for science education." *Science Education* 85, no.1 (January): 50-67.

Crane, Tim. "Aristotle Returns" (https://www.firstthings.com/article/2018/08/aristotle-returns).

Danticat, Edwige. 2015. "Sweet Micky and the Sad Deja Vu of Haiti's Presidential Elections." New Yorker, December 3, 2015.

Davis, Wade. 1997. *The Serpent and the Rainbow* Simon and Schuster, New York.

Descartes, Rene. 1969 *Discourse on Method* in *The Essential Descartes* Mentor Books, New York.

Dupre, Louis. 1966. *The Philosophical Foundations of Marxism* Harcourt Brace & World, New York.

Eagleton, Terry. 2011. *The Great Philosophers: Marx.* London: Orion Publishing Group Ltd.

Edmonds, Ennis B. 2012. *Rastafari: A Very Short Introduction.* Oxford: Oxford University Press.

Engber, Daniel. 2017. "Daryl Bem Proved ESP is Real." Slate, May 17, 2017. https://slate.com/health-and-science/2017/06/daryl-bem-proved-esp-is-real-showed-science-is-broken.html

Epic of Gilgamesh. 1972. Trans. N.K. Sanders Penguin Books, London.

Feyerabend, Paul. 1988. *Against Method* Verso, New York.

Feyerabend, Paul. 2016. *Philosophy of Nature* Polity Press, Cambridge UK.

Frank, Dana. 2014. "The Thugocracy Next Door." Politico, February 27, 2014. https://www.politico.com/magazine/story/2014/02/honduras-the-thugocracy-ext-door-103883.

Gadamer, Hans Georg. 1975. *Truth and Method* Seabury Press, New York.

Garroute, Eva-Marie. 2006. "Defining 'Radical Indigenism' and Creating an American Indian Scholarship." In Culture, Power, and History: Studies in Critical Sociology, edited by Stephen J. Pfohl. Chicago: Haymarket Books. 169-195

Girard, Rene. 1999. *I See Satan Fall Like Lightning* Orbis Books, Maryknoll.

Green Mountain Collective. (https://theanarchistlibrary.org/library/anti-racist-action-the-green-mountain-anarchist-collective-black-bloc-tactics-communique)

Govier, Trudy. 2005. "The Logic of War" in *Contemporary Moral Issues.* McGrath Hill Ryerson, Toronto. 544-557

Harris, Sam. 2005. *The End of Faith: Religion, Terror, and the Future of Reason.* New York: W.W. Norton.

Hegel, GWF. 1967. *The Phenomenology of Mind.* Translated by J.B. Baillie. New York: Harper Torchbooks.

Heidegger, Martin. 1977. "The Question Concerning Technology." *In*

Martin Heidegger: Basic Writings, edited by David Farell Krell, New York: Harper & Row.

Heilbroner, Robert. 1992. *Twenty-First Century Capitalism*. Concord: House of Anansi Press.

Hochschild, Arlie Russell. 2016. "The Ecstatic Edge of Politics: Sociology and Donald Trump." *American Sociological Association* 45, no. 6 (November): 683-689.

Ives, Kim. 2010. Interview with Fmr. President Bill Clinton. "'We Made a Devil's Bargain': Fmr. President Clinton Apologizes for Trade Policies that Destroyed Haitian Rice Farming." *Democracy Now!* video, 38:17, April 1, 2010.

Kant, Immanuel. 1993. *Foundations of the Metaphysics of Morals* Trans. Lewis White Beck Mac Millan Publishing Company, New York.

Kiekhefer, Richard. 2000. *Magic in the Middle Ages* Cambridge University Press, Cambridge.

Kollerstrom, Nick. 1989. "Kepler's Belief in Astrology." In *History and Astrology: Clio and Urania Confer*, London: Unwin Paperbacks. 152-170.

Kolakowski, Leszek. 1968. *Toward a Marxist Humanism: Essays on the Left Today*, New York: Grove Press.

Latour, Bruno. 1987. *Science in Action: How to Follow Scientists and Engineers through Society*. Cambridge: Harvard University Press.

Laudan, Larry. 1983. "The Demise of the Demarcation Problem." In *Physics, Philosophy and Psychoanalysis: Essays in Honor of Adolf Grünbaum*, edited by Robert S. Cohen and Larry Laudan,. Dordrecht: D. Reidel Publishing Company. 111-127

Lawrence, Marilynn. "Hellenistic Astrology" in *Internet Encyclopedia of Philosophy*.

Lewis, C.S. 1960. *The Four Loves*. Harper Collins, New York.

Luck, Georg, 2006 *Arcana Mundi* Johns Hopkins University Press, Baltimore.

Malebranche, 1992 *Philosophical Selections* Hackett Publishing, Indianapolis.

Marx, Karl, and Friedrich Engels. 1969. "Manifesto of the Communist

Party." In *Marx-Engels Selected Works*, Volume 1, 98-137. Moscow: Progress Publishers.

——. 1970. *The German Ideology*. Edited by C.J. Arthur. New York: International Publishers.

Mingardi, A. "A Sphere Around the Person" https://papers.ssrn.com/sol3/papers.cfm?abstract_id=910946

Murphey, Tom. 2015. "Land and Sea: Fairies." CBC video, 21:58, October 12, 2015. http://www.cbc.ca/player/play/2676901733

Murrell, Nathaniel S., William D. Spencer, and Adrian A. McFarlane. 1998. *Chanting Down Babylon: The Rastafari Reader*. Philadelphia: Temple University Press.

—— Chavanes, Barry "Rastafari and the Exorcism of the Ideology of Racism and Classism in Jamaica" 55-71

—— Chisholm, Clinton "The Rasta- Selassie-Ethiopian Connections" 166-177

—— Imani, Tafari-Ama "Rastawoman as Rebel: Case studies in Jamaica" 89-106

——McFarlane, A.A. "The Epistemological Significance of I-an-I" 107-124

——Murrell and Williams "The Black Biblical Hermeneutics of Rastafari" 326-348

Myers, PZ. 2007. "FFRF recap: heroes of the revolution, Hitchens screws the pooch, and the unbearable stodginess of atheists." Freethought Blogs, October 14, 2007. https://freethoughtblogs.com/pharyngula/2007/10/14/ffrf-recap/# ixzz5BAp6op6m

Nietzsche, Friedrich. 1989. *On the Genealogy of Morals* Vintage Books, New York.

Nietzsche, Friedrich. 1968. *Twilight of the Idols* in *The Portable Nietzsche* Penguin Books, London.

——. *The Gay Science*

Parmenides 1995, "The Way of Truth" in *A Pre-Socratics Reader* Hackett Publishing, Indianapolis.

Plato. 1961. *Republic* in *Collected Dialogues*. Bollingen Series, Princeton University Press, Princeton.

Plotinus. 1991. *Enneads* Trans. Stephen MacKenna. Penguin Classics, London.

Pierce, C.S. 1958. *Values in a Universe of Chance: Selected Writings* Double Day Anchor Books, New York.

Presents of God ministry. n.d. "Pope Wrote Koran!" Access date. http://www.remnantofgod.org/PopeKoran.htm

Pulver, Matthew. 2015. "Bill and Hillary's hyper-capitalist disaster: How the Clintons can apologize for a decade of deadly policies." Salon, May 5, 2015.

Quine, Willard Van Orman. 2011. "Two Dogmas of Empiricism" in *From Plato to Derrida* Prentice Hall, Boston. 1192-1206

Reno, Robert "Why I'm Anti-Anti-Trump" https://www.firstthings.com/blogs/firstthoughts/2016/05/why-im-anti-anti-trump)

Rossi and Le Grice. 2018. *Jung on Astrology* Routledge, London.

Said, Edward W. 2000 "Islam as News" from *The Edward Said Reader* Vintage Books, New York. 170-194

Sartre, Jean-Paul. 1975. "Portrait of an Anti-Semite" in *Existentialism from Dostoevsky to Sartre* Plume Books, New York.

Schafer, Arthur. https://umanitoba.ca/faculties/arts/departments/philosophy/ethics/media/Drug_Trial.pdf

Sidney, Phillip. 1982. *Silver Poets of the Sixteenth Century* Everyman Books, London.

Shakespeare, William. 1993. *A Midsummer Night's Dream* Washington Square Press, New York.

Shermer, Michael. 2002. *Why People Believe Weird Things: Pseudoscience, Superstition, and Other Confusions of Our Time.* New York: Holt Paperbacks.

http://skepticalsounds.blogspot.ca/2013/02/refuting-astrology.html.

Spielvogel, Jackson J. 2005. *Hitler and Nazi Germany.* Upper Saddle

River: Pearson Prentice Hall.

Tailor, Bob. 2015. "There's no such things as 'moderate' Islam, only moderate Muslims." Communities Digital News, August 31, 2015.

http://www.telegraph.co.uk/news/uknews/1439101/Astrologers-fail-to-predict-proof-they-are-wrong.html

Thagard, Paul R. 1978. "Why Astrology is a Pseudoscience." PSA: *Proceedings of the Biennial*
Meeting of the Philosophy of Science Association 1978, no. 1: 223-234.

The Atlantic. 2016. "'Hail Trump!': Richard Spencer Speech Excerpts." YouTube video, 3:07, November 21, 2016.
https://www.youtube.com/watch?v=1o6-bi3jlxk& t=108s.

The Religion of Peace. n.d. "Islam...What to Do?"
https://www.thereligionofpeace.com/pages/site/what-to-do.aspx

Thomas, Dylan. 1972. *Collected Poems* J.M Dent & Sons, London.

Tolkien, J.R.R. 2014. *On Fairy Stories.* Edited by Verlyn Flieger and Douglas A. Anderson. Glasgow: HarperCollins.

Virgil, 1982. *The Georgics* Trans. L.P. Wilkinson. Penguin Classics, London.

Zaimov, Stoyan. 2015. "Megachurch Pastor Robert Jeffress: Paris Attacks Prove Islam Inspired by Satan." Christian Post, November 17, 2015.

About the author

Dr. Bernard Wills teaches Humanities and Philosophy at Grenfell Campus Memorial University. He has degrees in Classics and Religious Studies from Dalhousie and McMaster. He has published a number of articles on Ancient, Medieval and Early Modern thought as well as occasional essays and poetry. Dr. Wills was born in Toronto but was raised on Cape Breton Island. He currently resides in Corner Brook NL. He can be contacted at bwills@swgc.mun.ca.

www.ingramcontent.com/pod-product-compliance
Lightning Source LLC
Chambersburg PA
CBHW051716090426
42738CB00010B/1933